# On Uncertain Graphs

# Synthesis Lectures on Data Management

Editor
**H.V. Jagadish**, *University of Michigan*

Founding Editor
**M. Tamer Özsu**, *University of Waterloo*

*Synthesis Lectures on Data Management* is edited by H.V. Jagadish of the University of Michigan. The series publishes 80–150 page publications on topics pertaining to data management. Topics include query languages, database system architectures, transaction management, data warehousing, XML and databases, data stream systems, wide scale data distribution, multimedia data management, data mining, and related subjects.

On Uncertain Graphs
Arijit Khan, Yuan Ye, and Lei Chen
2018

Answering Queries Using Views
Foto Afrati and Rada Chirkova
2017

Databases on Modern Hardware: How to Stop Underutilization and Love Multicores
Anatasia Ailamaki, Erieta Liarou, Pınar Tözün, Danica Porobic, and Iraklis Psaroudakis
2017

Instant Recovery with Write-Ahead Logging: Page Repair, System Restart, Media Restore, and System Failover, Second Edition
Goetz Graefe, Wey Guy, and Caetano Sauer
2016

Generating Plans from Proofs: The Interpolation-based Approach to Query Reformulation
Michael Benedikt, Julien Leblay, Balder ten Cate, and Efthymia Tsamoura
2016

iv

Veracity of Data: From Truth Discovery Computation Algorithms to Models of Misinformation Dynamics
Laure Berti-Équille and Javier Borge-Holthoefer
2015

Datalog and Logic Databases
Sergio Greco and Cristina Molinaro
2015

Big Data Integration
Xin Luna Dong and Divesh Srivastava
2015

Instant Recovery with Write-Ahead Logging: Page Repair, System Restart, and Media Restore
Goetz Graefe, Wey Guy, and Caetano Sauer
2014

Similarity Joins in Relational Database Systems
Nikolaus Augsten and Michael H. Böhlen
2013

Information and Influence Propagation in Social Networks
Wei Chen, Laks V.S. Lakshmanan, and Carlos Castillo
2013

Data Cleaning: A Practical Perspective
Venkatesh Ganti and Anish Das Sarma
2013

Data Processing on FPGAs
Jens Teubner and Louis Woods
2013

Perspectives on Business Intelligence
Raymond T. Ng, Patricia C. Arocena, Denilson Barbosa, Giuseppe Carenini, Luiz Gomes, Jr., Stephan Jou, Rock Anthony Leung, Evangelos Milios, Renée J. Miller, John Mylopoulos, Rachel A. Pottinger, Frank Tompa, and Eric Yu
2013

Semantics Empowered Web 3.0: Managing Enterprise, Social, Sensor, and Cloud-based Data and Services for Advanced Applications
Amit Sheth and Krishnaprasad Thirunarayan
2012

Database Repairing and Consistent Query Answering
Leopoldo Bertossi
2011

Managing Event Information: Modeling, Retrieval, and Applications
Amarnath Gupta and Ramesh Jain
2011

Fundamentals of Physical Design and Query Compilation
David Toman and Grant Weddell
2011

Methods for Mining and Summarizing Text Conversations
Giuseppe Carenini, Gabriel Murray, and Raymond Ng
2011

Probabilistic Databases
Dan Suciu, Dan Olteanu, Christopher Ré, and Christoph Koch
2011

Peer-to-Peer Data Management
Karl Aberer
2011

Probabilistic Ranking Techniques in Relational Databases
Ihab F. Ilyas and Mohamed A. Soliman
2011

Uncertain Schema Matching
Avigdor Gal
2011

Fundamentals of Object Databases: Object-Oriented and Object-Relational Design
Suzanne W. Dietrich and Susan D. Urban
2010

Advanced Metasearch Engine Technology
Weiyi Meng and Clement T. Yu
2010

Web Page Recommendation Models: Theory and Algorithms
Sule Gündüz-Ögüdücü
2010

Multidimensional Databases and Data Warehousing
Christian S. Jensen, Torben Bach Pedersen, and Christian Thomsen
2010

Management in the Cloud: Challenges and Opportunities
akant Agrawal, Sudipto Das, and Amr El Abbadi
2

Query Processing over Uncertain Databases
Lei Chen and Xiang Lian
2012

Foundations of Data Quality Management
Wenfei Fan and Floris Geerts
2012

Incomplete Data and Data Dependencies in Relational Databases
Sergio Greco, Cristian Molinaro, and Francesca Spezzano
2012

Business Processes: A Database Perspective
Daniel Deutch and Tova Milo
2012

Data Protection from Insider Threats
Elisa Bertino
2012

Deep Web Query Interface Understanding and Integration
Eduard C. Dragut, Weiyi Meng, and Clement T. Yu
2012

P2P Techniques for Decentralized Applications
Esther Pacitti, Reza Akbarinia, and Manal El-Dick
2012

Query Answer Authentication
HweeHwa Pang and Kian-Lee Tan
2012

Declarative Networking
Boon Thau Loo and Wenchao Zhou
2012

Full-Text (Substring) Indexes in External Memory
Marina Barsky, Ulrike Stege, and Alex Thomo
2011

Spatial Data Management
Nikos Mamoulis
2011

Database Replication
Bettina Kemme, Ricardo Jimenez-Peris, and Marta Patino-Martinez
2010

Relational and XML Data Exchange
Marcelo Arenas, Pablo Barcelo, Leonid Libkin, and Filip Murlak
2010

User-Centered Data Management
Tiziana Catarci, Alan Dix, Stephen Kimani, and Giuseppe Santucci
2010

Data Stream Management
Lukasz Golab and M. Tamer Özsu
2010

Access Control in Data Management Systems
Elena Ferrari
2010

An Introduction to Duplicate Detection
Felix Naumann and Melanie Herschel
2010

Privacy-Preserving Data Publishing: An Overview
Raymond Chi-Wing Wong and Ada Wai-Chee Fu
2010

Keyword Search in Databases
Jeffrey Xu Yu, Lu Qin, and Lijun Chang
2009

On Uncertain Graphs

Arijit Khan, Yuan Ye, and Lei Chen

ISBN: 978-3-031-00732-3      paperback
ISBN: 978-3-031-01860-2      ebook
ISBN: 978-3-031-00087-4      hardcover

DOI 10.1007/978-3-031-01860-2

A Publication in the Springer series
*SYNTHESIS LECTURES ON DATA MANAGEMENT*

Lecture #48
Series Editor: H.V. Jagadish, *University of Michigan*
Founding Editor: M. Tamer Özsu, *University of Waterloo*
Series ISSN
Print 2153-5418    Electronic 2153-5426

# On Uncertain Graphs

Arijit Khan
Nanyang Technological University, Singapore

Yuan Ye
Northeastern University, China

Lei Chen
Hong Kong University of Science and Technology, Hong Kong

*SYNTHESIS LECTURES ON DATA MANAGEMENT #48*

# ABSTRACT

Large-scale, highly interconnected networks, which are often modeled as graphs, pervade both our society and the natural world around us. Uncertainty, on the other hand, is inherent in the underlying data due to a variety of reasons, such as noisy measurements, lack of precise information needs, inference and prediction models, or explicit manipulation, e.g., for privacy purposes. Therefore, uncertain, or probabilistic, graphs are increasingly used to represent noisy linked data in many emerging application scenarios, and they have recently become a hot topic in the database and data mining communities. Many classical algorithms such as reachability and shortest path queries become #$\mathbf{P}$-complete and, thus, more expensive over uncertain graphs. Moreover, various complex queries and analytics are also emerging over uncertain networks, such as pattern matching, information diffusion, and influence maximization queries. In this book, we discuss the sources of uncertain graphs and their applications, uncertainty modeling, as well as the complexities and algorithmic advances on uncertain graphs processing in the context of both classical and emerging graph queries and analytics. We emphasize the current challenges and highlight some future research directions.

# KEYWORDS

uncertain graphs, reliability, pattern matching, similarity search, influence maximization

# Contents

**Acknowledgments** . . . . . . . . . . . . . . . . . . . . . . . . . . . . . . . . . . . . . . . . . . . **xiii**

**1  Introduction to Uncertain Graphs** . . . . . . . . . . . . . . . . . . . . . . . . . . . . . . **1**
    1.1  Data as Uncertain Graphs . . . . . . . . . . . . . . . . . . . . . . . . . . . . . . 1
    1.2  Modeling of Uncertain Graphs . . . . . . . . . . . . . . . . . . . . . . . . . . . 5
    1.3  Challenges in Processing Uncertain Graphs . . . . . . . . . . . . . . . . . . . 7

**2  Reliability Queries** . . . . . . . . . . . . . . . . . . . . . . . . . . . . . . . . . . . . . . . . **11**
    2.1  Reliability . . . . . . . . . . . . . . . . . . . . . . . . . . . . . . . . . . . . . . . . . 11
    2.2  Shortest Path . . . . . . . . . . . . . . . . . . . . . . . . . . . . . . . . . . . . . . 19
    2.3  Nearest Neighbors . . . . . . . . . . . . . . . . . . . . . . . . . . . . . . . . . . . 21

**3  Graph Pattern Matching Queries** . . . . . . . . . . . . . . . . . . . . . . . . . . . . . **25**
    3.1  The Pattern Matching Problem . . . . . . . . . . . . . . . . . . . . . . . . . . . 25
    3.2  Filtering-and-Verification Framework . . . . . . . . . . . . . . . . . . . . . . 27
    3.3  Probabilistic Pruning . . . . . . . . . . . . . . . . . . . . . . . . . . . . . . . . . 28
    3.4  Verification . . . . . . . . . . . . . . . . . . . . . . . . . . . . . . . . . . . . . . . . 31
        3.4.1  Basic Sampling . . . . . . . . . . . . . . . . . . . . . . . . . . . . . . . 32
        3.4.2  Tree-based Sampling . . . . . . . . . . . . . . . . . . . . . . . . . . . 32
        3.4.3  Hybrid Sampling . . . . . . . . . . . . . . . . . . . . . . . . . . . . . . 33

**4  Graph Similarity Search Queries** . . . . . . . . . . . . . . . . . . . . . . . . . . . . . . **37**
    4.1  The Similarity Search Problem . . . . . . . . . . . . . . . . . . . . . . . . . . . 37
    4.2  Probabilistic Subgraph Similarity Query Processing . . . . . . . . . . . . . 41
    4.3  Probabilistic Supergraph Similarity Query Processing . . . . . . . . . . . . 47

**5  Influence Maximization** . . . . . . . . . . . . . . . . . . . . . . . . . . . . . . . . . . . . **55**
    5.1  Information Diffusion Models . . . . . . . . . . . . . . . . . . . . . . . . . . . . 55
    5.2  The Influence Maximization Problem . . . . . . . . . . . . . . . . . . . . . . . 56
    5.3  Competitive Influence Maximization . . . . . . . . . . . . . . . . . . . . . . . 58
    5.4  Influence Maximization as a Service . . . . . . . . . . . . . . . . . . . . . . . . 59
    5.5  Topic-aware Influence Maximization . . . . . . . . . . . . . . . . . . . . . . . 60

**6  Major Open Problems** . . . . . . . . . . . . . . . . . . . . . . . . . . . . . . . . . . . . . . . . . . . . 63

**Bibliography** . . . . . . . . . . . . . . . . . . . . . . . . . . . . . . . . . . . . . . . . . . . . . . . . . . . . 65

**Authors' Biographies** . . . . . . . . . . . . . . . . . . . . . . . . . . . . . . . . . . . . . . . . . . . 79

# Acknowledgments

We would like to thank our families for their love and support during the busy time spent in writing this book.

For their collaborations, Arijit Khan would like to thank Xifeng Yan, Donald Kossmann, Charu Aggarwal, Francesco Bonchi, Gustavo Alonso, Aris Gionis, Sameh Elnikety, Chengkai Li, Gao Cong, Sourav Bhowmick, Lei Chen, Cong Yu, Prasenjit Mitra, Shu Tao, Yinghui Wu, Francesco Gullo, Aamir Cheema, Vishwakarma Singh, Xiangyu Ke, Leroy Lim Hong Quan, Siyuan Liu, Pratanu Roy, Lorenzo Severini, Vijaya Krishna Yalavarthi, Sixing Yan, Tenindra Abeywickrama, Michelle Teo Wan Teng, Rojin Rezvan, Andreas Nufer, Gustavo Segovia, Thomas Wohler, Benjamin Zehnder, Bojana Dimcheva, and Nandish Jayaram.

The research of Arijit Khan is supported by AcRF MOE Tier-1 RG83/16 and NTU M4081678. Any opinions, findings, and conclusions in this publication are those of the authors and do not necessarily reflect the views of the funding agencies.

Sincerely,


Arijit Khan, Yuan Ye, and Lei Chen
July 2018

CHAPTER 1

# Introduction to Uncertain Graphs

## 1.1 DATA AS UNCERTAIN GRAPHS

*"The real world is always certain; it is our knowledge of it that is sometimes uncertain."*
—Amihai Motro [Management of Uncertainty in Database Systems]

With the advent of the Internet and the mobile technology, availability of network data has increased dramatically, including the World Wide Web, social networks, information networks, traffic networks, genome databases, knowledge graphs, and medical and government records. Such data are often represented as attributed graphs, where nodes are entities and edges represent relations among these entities. However, uncertainty is evident in graph data due to a variety of reasons, such as noisy measurements [Aggarwal, 2009], inconsistent, incorrect, and possibly ambiguous information sources [Chen and Wang, 2014], lack of precise information needs [Zhou et al., 2010], inference and prediction models [Adar and Re, 2007, L.-Nowell and Kleinberg, 2003], or explicit manipulation, e.g., for privacy purposes [Boldi et al., 2012]. In these cases, data is represented as an uncertain graph; that is, a graph whose nodes, edges, and attributes are accompanied with a probability of existence. In Figure 1.1, we show a sensor network modeled as an uncertain graph, where the uncertainty on an edge denotes the packet delivery probability via the corresponding link. With the popularity of uncertain data, uncertain graphs are increasingly becoming important in many emerging domains including biological networks [Sevon et al., 2006], knowledge bases [Bollacker et al., 2008], social networks [Zou et al., 2010a], influence maximization [Kempe et al., 2003], road networks [Hua and Pei, 2010a], crowd sourcing [Wang et al., 2012], among many others. Below we discuss some real-world applications of uncertain graphs.

**Biological Networks.** In protein-protein interaction networks [Krogan et al., 2006], nodes represent proteins and edges represent interactions among them. Interactions are established for a limited number of proteins, through noisy and error-prone experiments. Thus, each edge is typically associated with a probability accounting for the existence of the interaction (Figure 1.2). Many uncertain biological networks are indeed available from String [CPR et al.], BioMine [of Helsinki], and NCBI [for Biotechnology Information] databases. In this context, predicting co-complex memberships [Asthana et al., 2004, Krogan et al., 2006] and new interactions [Potamias et al., 2010, Sevon et al., 2006] require computing classical graph algorithms such as

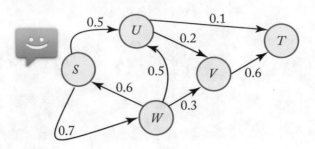

Figure 1.1: Sensor network as an uncertain graph. The edge probability denotes the packet delivery probability via the corresponding link.

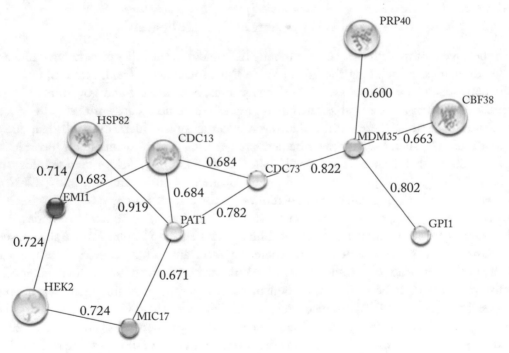

Figure 1.2: Interaction network of Mic17 obtained from the STRING database [CPR et al.]. All interactions (i.e., uncertain edges) are derived from experimental evidences.

reachability [Jin et al., 2011b, Khan et al., 2014, Zhu et al., 2011], shortest paths [Frank, 1969, Yuan et al., 2010, Zou et al., 2011], nearest neighbors [Potamias et al., 2010], clustering [Liu et al., 2012], maximal cliques [Zou et al., 2010b], and dense subgraphs finding [Liu et al., 2011] over uncertain graphs.

**Knowledge Bases.** A knowledge base stores entities and their relationships in a machine-readable format to help computers understand human information and queries [Chen and Wang, 2014]. Examples of knowledge bases include the Google knowledge graph [Blog, 2012], Freebase [Bollacker et al., 2008], DBPedia [Auer et al., 2007], Probase [Wu et al., 2012], Yago [Suchanek et al., 2007], and DeepDive [Shin et al., 2015]. Uncertainty is inherent in knowledge bases due to many reasons such as knowledge extraction using statistical models, incorrect and conflicting data sources, derived facts and query results, NULL values in databases, and majority voting in crowdsourced information. In addition, the query graph itself can be uncertain because the users are often unaware about their precise information needs [Zhou et al., 2010]. Hence, there is a growing interest for methods that can represent and query uncertain knowledge bases [Chen and Wang, 2010, Huang and Liu, 2009, Lian and Chen, 2011, Yuan et al., 2012].

**Social Networks.** With the popularity of online social networks, they have become indispensable in various critical application settings such as recommendation, trend detection, expert finding, public health community building, and terrorist activity prediction. Uncertainty arises in social network data due to noisy data collection and integration policy, massive size of the networks, missing attributes, as well as due to privacy and anonymization purposes [Adar and Re, 2007]. Thus, one needs to perform complex data mining operations, e.g., frequent subgraphs mining [Papapetrou et al., 2011, Zou et al., 2009c, 2010a,c], classification [Dallachiesa et al., 2014, Kong et al., 2013], core decomposition [Bonchi et al., 2014], highly reliable subgraphs finding [Jin et al., 2011a], link prediction [Taranto et al., 2012], and subgraph pattern matching [Li et al., 2014, Yuan et al., 2011] over uncertain social networks.

**Viral Marketing.** Viral marketing, also known as the word-of-mouth recommendation, refers to marketing techniques that use social networking services to increase the brand awareness or to achieve higher product sales through self-replicating viral processes, analogous to the spread of viruses or computer viruses. A well-studied problem in this context is the influence maximization [Domingos and Richardson, 2001, Kempe et al., 2003] that models the influence of a user $u$ to another user $v$ as a probability value on the edge $(u, v)$, as depicted in Figure 1.3. The problem aims at finding a set of seed nodes that generates the largest expected information cascade in a social network. Viral marketing and influence maximization are gradually becoming hot topics in the database and data mining research community that require extensive modeling of information cascade over uncertain graphs.

**Road Networks.** Modeling and analysis of road networks has significant applications in a number of scientific domains including traffic management and congestion control, evacuation planning, and location-aware recommendation services. Road networks data are often modeled as uncertain graphs, where the properties of edges and nodes are probabilistic and usually modeled as stochastic functions of time [Foschini et al., 2011, Hu et al., 2018, Hua and Pei, 2010a]. In Figure 1.4, we show a road network with edge weight and uncertainty: Edge weight represents the normal travel time and the uncertainty denotes the probability of not having a traffic congestion along that road segment. Management and querying of such graph data is a chal-

Figure 1.3: Probability of an edge $(u, v)$ in a social network represents the likelihood that some action of user $u$ will be adopted by her follower $v$.

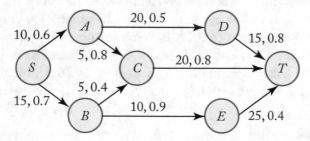

Figure 1.4: Road network with edge weight and uncertainty: Edge weight denotes the normal travel time and the uncertainty defines the probability of not having a traffic congestion along that road segment.

lenging problem, e.g., finding the shortest route from one place to another, or a search for the nearest restaurant would depend not only on the structure of the network, but also on other time-dependent properties such as the congestion probability on certain road segments at a specific time of the day.

**Wireless and Mobile Networks.** With the advent of wireless technologies and miniaturized hardware, pervasive computing has become quite prevalent. There are several algorithmic issues in pervasive computing such as effective deployment of sensors, maintaining coverage and connectivity, channel sharing, energy-efficient routing and data-aggregation, which are often modeled as uncertain graph problems. As an example, in mobile ad hoc networks, the connectivity between nodes is estimated using noisy measurements, thus leading to links naturally associated with a probability of existence (Figure 1.1). In these networks, the notion of "delivery probability" is usually exploited to determine the nodes for which the probability of receiving a packet by another node in the network is adequately high [Ghosh et al., 2007].

In an uncertain, or probabilistic, graph, uncertainty can be associated with any one or multiple of the following components.

**Edge Uncertainty.** Edge uncertainty has been widely studied in the literature of uncertain graphs. It denotes the probability of existence of a link between the two corresponding nodes. In addition to noise, measurement errors, inference and prediction models etc. which result in edge uncertainty, edge probability can also be associated with various edge attributes [Barbieri et al., 2012]. As an example, Lady Gaga would have more influence on her followers for music and fashion-related tweets, but Barack Obama would have more influence on his followers for politics-based tweets.

**Node Uncertainty.** Node uncertainty has been considered mainly in the context of device networks and graph pattern matching queries. While the most common interpretation of node uncertainty is to denote its existence probability, e.g., Yuan et al. [2011] and Moustafa et al. [2014] introduced the notion of *identity uncertainty*, that is, uncertainty about whether each real world entity is represented by one or multiple nodes in the graph.

**Attribute Uncertainty.** Attribute uncertainty defines uncertainty about the attribute values of nodes and edges, and it has been used in the context of graph pattern matching, uncertain query graph formulation, and processing of RDF queries.

Due to wide availability and potential applications of uncertain graphs, it is important to explicitly model uncertainty, together with state-of-the-art algorithms and systems for large graphs processing. One might think of various naïve approaches, e.g., considering edge probabilities as weights. However, edge probabilities are semantically different from edge weights, and there is no meaningful way to perform such a casting. One can also set a threshold probability value and decide to ignore any component with an existence probability below that threshold. Unfortunately, there is no principled way of deciding what the right value of the threshold is, and it might require domain expertise. Besides, in reality, we are often interested in the probability that a certain property holds, rather than a binary yes/no answer, e.g., finding the reliability of a system, or the packet delivery probability over a sensor networks. In all such cases, it is important to explicitly deal with uncertainty.

## 1.2 MODELING OF UNCERTAIN GRAPHS

**Independent Probabilities.** The bulk of the literature on uncertain graphs assumes the existence of the components in the graph independent from one another, and interprets uncertain graphs according to the well-known *possible-world semantics* [Jin et al., 2011b, Potamias et al., 2010, Zhu et al., 2011]. For example, an uncertain graph with $m$ edges and the probabilities assigned on edges yields $2^m$ possible deterministic graphs, which are derived by sampling independently each edge with its corresponding probability.

We can model such an uncertain graph $\mathcal{G}$ with a triple $(V, E, p)$, where $V$ is a set of $n$ nodes, $E \subseteq V \times V$ is a set of $m$ directed edges, and $p : E \rightarrow (0, 1]$ is a probability function that assigns a probability of existence to each edge in $E$. A possible graph $G \sqsubseteq \mathcal{G}$ is a pair $(V, E_G)$, where $E_G \subseteq E$, and its sampling probability is:

$$\Pr(G) = \prod_{e \in E_G} p(e) \prod_{e' \in E \setminus E_G} (1 - p(e')). \tag{1.1}$$

Figure 1.5 illustrates one uncertain graph with two edges and its $2^2 = 4$ possible worlds. One may note that the probabilities of the existence of all possible worlds add up to 1.

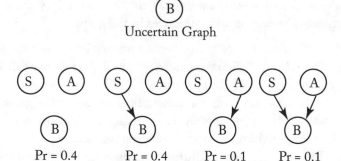

Figure 1.5: Independent probability and possible world semantics.

**Correlated Probabilities.** While the independent model discussed above is one of the simplest possible ways to deal with uncertainty in graph databases, it naturally ignores the correlations among various graph components. For example, in a traffic network, if a road is crowded at a certain point of time, most likely the road in the next intersection would also be crowded. The independent model fails to consider these relationships. There are several works that model such correlations with conditional probabilities (e.g., Collins and Smith [2014], Moustafa et al. [2014], Potamias et al. [2010]); however, this also incurs additional complexity in the problem.

In Figure 1.6, we demonstrate an uncertain graph with conditional edge probabilities, where the existence of an outgoing edge from a node depends on the existence of incoming edges to that node. One can represent such probabilities with a *conditional probability table*. If the underlying graph is a directed acyclic graph (DAG), generating independent samples are relatively easier. One needs to sample the edges of $\mathcal{G}$ in their topological order. However, complexity arises if $\mathcal{G}$ has cycles. In such cases, one may employ Gibbs sampling, a Markov Chain Monte Carlo (MCMC) technique [Bishop, 2006] to generate independent samples.

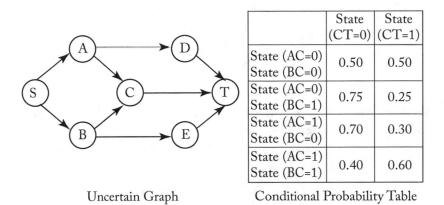

| | State (CT=0) | State (CT=1) |
|---|---|---|
| State (AC=0) State (BC=0) | 0.50 | 0.50 |
| State (AC=0) State (BC=1) | 0.75 | 0.25 |
| State (AC=1) State (BC=0) | 0.70 | 0.30 |
| State (AC=1) State (BC=1) | 0.40 | 0.60 |

Uncertain Graph                    Conditional Probability Table

Figure 1.6: Correlated probability and conditional probability table.

## 1.3    CHALLENGES IN PROCESSING UNCERTAIN GRAPHS

The challenges in uncertain graphs processing are both semantics and computation driven. From the perspective of the semantics, there is no uniform model of uncertain graphs; rather assignment and interpretation of the probabilities must be application specific. We illustrate this point with two popular graph operations.

**Shortest Path.** How can we define the shortest path between two nodes in an uncertain graph? The definition could depend on the application and the specific uncertainty semantics. Therefore, the techniques for computing the shortest path would also vary. As depicted in Potamias et al. [2010], the traditional shortest path (in a certain graph) or even the most probable path might not be the best candidate for the shortest path over an uncertain graph. Let us assume that all edges have weight 1 in the uncertain graph ($\mathcal{G}$) in Figure 1.7, whereas the corresponding edge probabilities are also shown in the figure. If $\mathcal{G}$ were a certain graph, the shortest path from $S$ to $T$ would have been the direct edge from $S$ to $T$. However, this edge has a small probability in $\mathcal{G}$. On the other hand, the most probable path from $S$ to $T$ in $\mathcal{G}$ is $SB_1 B_2 \ldots B_r T$ (with probability 1). However, the probability that this is indeed the shortest path is very small, because the path $SAT$ of length only 2 exists with a very high probability, i.e., $(1 - \epsilon)^2$.

Therefore, Zou et al. [2011] defines the *shortest path probability*, $SP(P)$ of a path $P$ as the probability that $P$ is indeed a shortest path in the possible worlds of the uncertain graph $\mathcal{G}$.

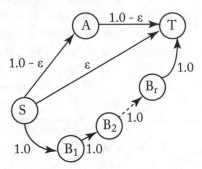

Figure 1.7: Shortest path over uncertain graph. We assume independent edge probabilities and $\epsilon$ is a very small probability value.

Formally,

$$SP(P) = \sum_{G \sqsubseteq \mathcal{G}} I_{SP}(G, P) \times \Pr(G). \qquad (1.2)$$

In Equation (1.2), $I_{SP}(G)$ is an indicator function that takes value 1 if $P$ is a shortest path from $S$ to $T$ in the possible world $G$, and 0 otherwise. Based on this definition, Zou et al. [2011] formulates the problem of identifying the top-$k$ paths from $S$ to $T$ with the highest shortest path probabilities, whereas Yuan et al. [2010] proposes to find all paths with the shortest path probability more than a pre-defined threshold. In addition, various shortest path distance metrics such as median distance, majority distance, and expected reliable distance were defined in Potamias et al. [2010].

**Frequent Subgraphs Mining.** The traditional definition of support (e.g., the number of occurrences) does not hold for frequent subgraph mining over uncertain graph databases. In Figure 1.8, we show a graph database with 6 uncertain graphs. If one does not consider the edge probabilities, the subgraph ABC (with a triangle shape) has support 6, since it occurs in all 6 graphs. However, in reality, we might not consider ABC a frequent subgraph because its edges have small probabilities. To formalize this notion, Zou et al. [2009c] proposes *expected support*, which is defined below.

Given an uncertain graph database $\mathcal{D} = \{\mathcal{G}_1, \mathcal{G}_2, \ldots, \mathcal{G}_r\}$, a certain instance $D = \{G_1, G_2, \ldots, G_r\}$ of $\mathcal{D}$ consists of possible worlds of these uncertain graphs, i.e., $G_i \sqsubseteq \mathcal{G}_i$ for all $i \in (1, r)$. This is denoted as $D \sqsubseteq \mathcal{D}$ and its probability is given by:

$$\Pr(D) = \prod_{i \in (1,r)} \Pr(G_i). \qquad (1.3)$$

The expected support of a subgraph $g$ is defined as follows:

$$ES(g) = \sum_{D \sqsubseteq \mathcal{D}} S(D, g) \times \Pr(D). \qquad (1.4)$$

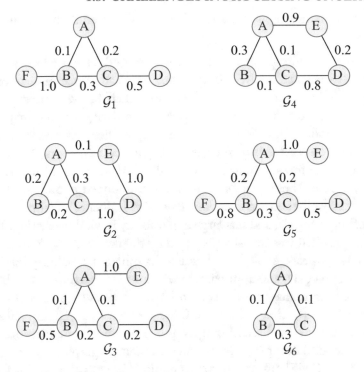

Figure 1.8: Frequent subgraph mining over uncertain graph databases.

In Equation (1.4), $S(D, g)$ denotes the support of $g$ in $D$ in the classical way, i.e., the number of occurrences of $g$ in the certain graph database $D$. One can verify that the expected support of subgraph ABC is only 0.038 by this definition.

It is important to note that even if two subgraphs have the same expected support, one might not be equally certain that they are frequent. For example, both the edges AE and CD have expected support 3; however, we can be more certain that AE occurs at least 3 times in a possible instance of the uncertain database. This is because the probability associated with AE are either close to 0 or 1. To define this concept, Renz et al. [2009] introduces *frequentness probability*, which is the probability that the support of a subgraph is larger than a predefined threshold. Thus, as one considers different semantics of frequent subgraphs, their mining techniques would also vary.

From the computation perspective, while many graph algorithms such as subgraph isomorphism are intrinsically hard, even the simplest graph algorithms such as reachability and shortest path queries become #**P**-complete and, hence, more expensive over uncertain graphs. Therefore, exact computation is almost infeasible for today's large-scale graph data and focus nowadays is toward designing approximation algorithms with efficient sampling, indexing, and filtering strategies.

**Book Outline.** The uncertain graph models have been studied since 1970's in the context of device networks [Aggarwal et al., 1975]. In this book, we shall primarily focus on database-style queries and analytics over uncertain graphs, including reachability, shortest paths, and nearest neighbors (Chapter 2), pattern matching (Chapter 3), similarity search (Chapter 4), and influence maximization (Chapter 5), which have seen an unprecedented interest in the last ten years. The first three chapters on reachability, shortest paths, nearest neighbors, pattern matching, and similarity search (i.e., Chapters 2, 3, and 4) generally deal with online, ad hoc queries, which require fast response time. These queries are useful in the context of biological, social, communication, transport, as well as in information networks. Influence maximization, discussed in Chapter 5, is an offline analysis, and has large applicability in viral marketing. While the influence maximization problem was initially proposed by the data mining community [Domingos and Richardson, 2001, Kempe et al., 2003], due to its inherent scalability bottlenecks, designing of more efficient, practical, and approximate solutions for this difficult problem has become quite popular in the data management research [Arora et al., 2017, Aslay et al., 2014, Chen et al., 2015, Ke et al., 2018, Li et al., 2015b, Ohsaka et al., 2016, Tang et al., 2015]. Finally, we shall conclude this book by discussing open problems and future directions in Chapter 6. Interested readers may find other relevant works on uncertain graphs, such as graph generative models [Leskovec et al., 2005], uncertain graphs mining [Bonchi et al., 2014, Dallachiesa et al., 2014, Kassiano et al., 2017, Liu et al., 2012, Zou et al., 2009b], uncertain databases [Aggarwal and Yu, 2009, Suciu et al., 2011, Zhang et al., 2008], and probabilistic graphical models [Deshpande et al., 2009, Pearl, 1982] in recent surveys and books.

# SUMMARY

In this chapter we briefly discussed sources and applications of uncertain graphs, various uncertainty semantics, and their challenges.

# CHAPTER 2

# Reliability Queries

A fundamental class of problem in uncertain graphs is the so-called *reliability*, which asks to estimate the probability that two given (sets of) nodes are reachable. Reliability has been well-studied in the context of device networks (e.g., telecommunication networks), i.e., networks whose nodes are electronic devices and the (physical) links between such devices have a probability of failure [Aggarwal et al., 1975]. More recently, the attention has been shifted to other types of networks that can naturally be represented as uncertain graphs, such as social networks or biological networks [Jin et al., 2011b, Potamias et al., 2010, Zhu et al., 2011]. Existing reliability queries include computing the probability that two nodes are connected (*two-terminal reliability* [Aggarwal et al., 1975]), all nodes in the network are pairwise connected (*all-terminal reliability* [Sharafat and Ma'rouzi, 2009]), or all nodes in a given subset are pairwise connected (*k-terminal reliability* [Hardy et al., 2007]). In this chapter, we discuss two-terminal reliability and two other related queries, namely shortest paths and nearest neighbors over uncertain graphs. Unless otherwise specified, we shall consider probabilities on graph edges and assume that the existence of the edges is independent from one another.

## 2.1 RELIABILITY

An *uncertain graph* $\mathcal{G}$ is a triple $(V, E, p)$, where $V$ is a set of $n$ nodes, $E \subseteq V \times V$ is a set of $m$ directed edges, and $p : E \rightarrow (0, 1]$ is a probability function that assigns a probability of existence to each edge in $E$. An uncertain graph $\mathcal{G}$ with $m$ edges yields $2^m$ possible deterministic graphs, which are derived by sampling independently each edge $e \in E$ with probability $p(e)$. More precisely, a possible graph $G \sqsubseteq \mathcal{G}$ is a pair $(V, E_G)$, where $E_G \subseteq E$, and its sampling probability is:

$$\Pr(G) = \prod_{e \in E_G} p(e) \prod_{e' \in E \setminus E_G} (1 - p(e')). \tag{2.1}$$

For a possible deterministic graph $G$, we define an indicator function $I_G(s, t)$ to be 1 if there is a path in $G$ from a source node $s \in V$ to a target node $t \in V$, and 0 otherwise. The probability that $t$ is reachable from $s$ in the uncertain graph $\mathcal{G}$, denoted by $R(s, t)$, and defined as two-terminal reliability (or, $s$-$t$ reliability), is computed as:

$$R(s, t) = \sum_{G \sqsubseteq \mathcal{G}} I_G(s, t) \times \Pr(G). \tag{2.2}$$

**Theoretical Characterization.** The number of possible worlds $G \sqsubseteq \mathcal{G}$ is exponential in the number of edges, which makes the exact computation of $R(s, t)$ infeasible even for moderately sized graphs. As stated formally in Theorem 2.1, the problem is #**P**-complete.

**Theorem 2.1**    *The s–t reliability problem in an uncertain graph is #**P**-complete.*

The formal proof is given in Ball [1986]. We shall provide only a proof sketch in this chapter. Prior to that, we discuss the #**P**-complete class and its relation with other commonly used complexity classes including P, NP, and NP-complete. We start with a few definitions, primarily in the context of graphs.

• **Recognition Problem.** Given a graph $G = (V, E)$ together with node and/or edge weights, is there a subgraph of $G$ that satisfies property $X$?

The class P consists of those recognition problems for which polynomial-time algorithms exist. NP, on the other hand, is the class of recognition problems with the property that given a candidate subgraph, testing whether or not it satisfies property $X$ can be accomplished in polynomial time. Essentially, all problems in P are also in NP; however, it is not known if P = NP. We define those problems as NP-hard such that if a polynomial algorithm existed for one of them, then a polynomial algorithm would exist for all members in NP. A recognition problem is called NP-complete if this is both in NP as well as NP-hard. Clearly, NP-complete problems are the hardest problems in NP.

• **Counting Problem.** Given a graph $G = (V, E)$ together with node and/or edge weights, how many subgraphs of $G$ satisfy property $X$?

A complexity class of counting problems, similar to NP, has been defined. The class #**P** [Valiant, 1979] consists of counting problems with the property that given a candidate subgraph, testing whether or not it satisfies property $X$ can be accomplished in polynomial time. Clearly, the counting version of any problem in NP is in #**P**. As earlier, #**P**-hard consists of those problems such that if a polynomial algorithm exists for one of them, then a polynomial algorithm exists for all members of #**P**. #**P**-complete problems are hardest in #**P**, because in addition to being #**P**, they are also #**P**-hard. Since the counting version of a problem is at least as hard as the corresponding recognition problem, #**P**-complete problems are at least as hard as NP-complete problems. Therefore, *s–t* reliability problem, being #**P**-complete, is at least as hard, if not harder than NP-complete problems.

The proof of Theorem 2.1 follows by showing that (1) reliability computation is essentially a counting problem, and then (2) by deriving a polynomial-time reduction from the problem of finding the number of minimum cardinality *s–t*-cuts in a deterministic graph, which is #**P**-complete [Provan and Ball, 1983]. For simplicity, we assume an uncertain graph $\mathcal{G}$ where every edge can exist independent of others with a probability $p$. Then the *s–t* reliability can be computed as follows:

$$R(s, t) = \sum_{i=0}^{m} f_i \, p^{m-i} (1 - p)^i. \tag{2.3}$$

As noted earlier, $m$ is the number of edges in $\mathcal{G}$. $F = \langle f_1\ f_2\ \dots\ f_m \rangle$ is called the reliability polynomial. Each coefficient $f_i$ counts the number of subsets of edges of cardinality $i$ such that when a subset is deleted, there still remains a path from $s$ to $t$. This is essentially a counting problem. Given a subset of edges (i.e., one possible world of $\mathcal{G}$), one can determine in polynomial time if $t$ is reachable from $s$. Therefore, the problem is in #**P**. Next, we note that if we can determine all the coefficients of the reliability polynomial, then we immediately know the number of minimum cardinality $s$-$t$ cuts. This is because if the cardinality of a minimum cardinality $s$-$t$ cut is $c$, then for all $i < c$, $f_i = \binom{n}{i}$, and $f_c = \binom{n}{i} - n_c$, where $n_c$ is the number of the minimum cardinality $s$-$t$ cuts. However, as the problem of finding the number of minimum cardinality $s$-$t$-cuts is #**P**-complete, the problem of determining a general coefficient of the reliability polynomial is also #**P**-hard. The final part of the proof follows from the fact that if one can determine the $s$-$t$ reliability in polynomial time, then it is possible to find all the coefficients of the reliability polynomial by considering $m + 1$ different values of $p$ and then solving a system of $m + 1$ equations with $m + 1$ unknowns. Hence, the theorem follows.

It was further shown in Ball [1986] that the $s$-$t$ reliability problem remains #**P**-complete even for planar graphs and directed acyclic graphs (DAG). However, the problem can be solved in polynomial time over trees and series-parallel networks (Figure 2.1).

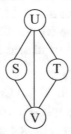

Figure 2.1: The graph is not series/parallel with respect to $S$ and $T$, but series/parallel with respect to $U$ and $V$.

**Exact Reliability Computation.** The exact reliability computation by enumerating all possible worlds of an uncertain graph requires exponential time to the number of edges, and this is infeasible even for moderately sized graphs.

Alternative methods are proposed in the literature for computing the exact reliability, e.g., pathsets and cutsets enumeration.

• **Pathset Enumeration.** An $s$-$t$-pathset is a minimal set of edges whose existence ensures a path from $s$ to $t$. Let us consider that the pathsets are denoted as $P_1, P_2, \dots, P_r$. Then, one can compute the reliability as given below:

$$R(s,t) = \Pr\left[\bigcup_{i=1}^{r} P_r\right]. \tag{2.4}$$

• **Cutset Enumeration.** An $s$-$t$-cutset is a minimal set of edges whose deletion leaves no path from $s$ to $t$. Let us assume that the cutsets are $C_1, C_2, \ldots, C_r$. Then, the reliability can be computed as follows:

$$R(s, t) = 1 - \Pr\left[\bigcup_{i=1}^{r} C_r\right]. \tag{2.5}$$

Unfortunately, the number of cutsets and pathsets in a graph can still be exponential to the number of nodes and edges. Besides, if one applies the inclusion-exclusion principle, the number of terms on the right-hand-side of Equations (2.4) and (2.5) would be $2^r$, i.e., exponential to the number of pathsets and cutsets, respectively. Nevertheless, for the $s$-$t$ reliability problem, Provan and Ball [1984] developed an algorithm of time complexity quadratic to the number of cutsets. Therefore, if the number of cutsets is small for some $s$ and $t$ nodes in a specific graph, then the exact $s$-$t$ reliability can be computed efficiently via cutsets enumeration.

Further research on reliability has considered polynomial-time upper/lower bounds, including Kruskal-Katona bound, polynomial-based, edge-packing-based, and cutset enumeration-based bounds [Brecht and Colbourn, 1988, Bulka and Dugan, 1994, Galtier et al., 2005]. However, due to the complexity of exact $s$-$t$ reliability computation, the focus nowadays has mainly been on approximate and heuristic solutions over large-scale networks [Fishman, 1986, Jin et al., 2011b, Khan et al., 2014, Potamias et al., 2010, Zhu et al., 2011, 2015]. In this context, we shall discuss the Monte Carlo sampling, as well as other sampling techniques improving upon the efficiency of classic Monte Carlo methods for $s$-$t$ reliability estimation.

**Monte Carlo Sampling.** In the basic Monte Carlo (MC) sampling, we first sample $K$ possible worlds $G_1, G_2, \ldots, G_K$ of the uncertain graph $\mathcal{G}$ according to independent edge probabilities. We then compute the reachability in each sampled graph $G_i$, and define $I_{G_i}(s, t) = 1$ if $t$ is reachable from $s$ in $G_i$, and 0 otherwise. Given this, we have the MC sampling estimator:

$$R(s, t) \approx \hat{R}(s, t) = \frac{1}{K} \sum_{i=1}^{K} I_{G_i}(s, t). \tag{2.6}$$

This is also known as the hit-and-miss Monte Carlo. The basic sampling estimator $\hat{R}(s, t)$ is an unbiased estimator of the $s$-$t$ reliability, i.e., $E(\hat{R}(s, t)) = R(s, t)$, and its variance can be determined due to Binomial distribution $\sim B(K, R(s, t))$ [Fishman, 1986, Jin et al., 2011b]:

$$Var\left(\hat{R}(s, t)\right) = \frac{1}{K} \cdot R(s, t) \cdot (1 - R(s, t)) \approx \frac{1}{K} \cdot \hat{R}(s, t) \cdot \left(1 - \hat{R}(s, t)\right). \tag{2.7}$$

It is possible to derive bounds on the number of MC samples needed to provide a good estimate for the $s$-$t$ reliability problem. In particular, it was shown in Potamias et al. [2010] by applying the Chernoff bound that with number of samples $K \geq \frac{3}{\epsilon^2 R(s,t)} \ln\left(\frac{2}{\lambda}\right)$, we can ensure the following:

$$\Pr\left(\left|\hat{R}(s,t) - R(s,t)\right| \geq \epsilon R(s,t)\right) \leq \lambda. \tag{2.8}$$

The time complexity to generate $K$ possible worlds is $\mathcal{O}(mK)$. In each possible world, the reachability can be determined by performing a breadth-first search (BFS) from the source node. Each BFS requires $\mathcal{O}(m + n)$ time. Therefore, the overall time complexity of MC sampling based reliability estimation is $\mathcal{O}(K(m + n))$. In essence, one may combine MC sampling with BFS from the source node for improved efficiency [Jin et al., 2011b, Khan et al., 2014]. It means that an edge in the current possible world is sampled only upon request. This avoids sampling of many edges in parts of the graph that are not reached with the current BFS, thus increasing the chance of an early termination.

**BFS Sharing for MC Sampling.** In practice, MC sampling can be inefficient over large-scale networks due to two reasons.

- For each $s$-$t$ reliability query, we need to generate $K$ possible worlds via sampling. Based on experimental evidences from state-of-the-art works [Jin et al., 2011a, Kempe et al., 2003, Potamias et al., 2010], $K$ can be in the order of thousands to achieve a reasonable accuracy. However, as correctly pointed out in Parchas et al. [2014] and Zhu et al. [2015], this sampling procedure does not contribute to the reliability estimation process directly. For example, one can pre-compute these $K$ possible worlds in an off-line manner to further improve the efficiency of online $s$-$t$ reliability estimation.

- There could be a significant overlap in structures of different possible worlds [Jin et al., 2011b, Zhu et al., 2011, 2015]. Unfortunately, the reliability estimation via basic MC sampling performs a separate BFS over each possible world, therefore it cannot take advantage of the common substructure across various possible worlds.

Zhu et al. [2015] perform an off-line sampling to generate $K$ possible worlds: $G_1, G_2, \ldots, G_K$. In order to minimize the storage overhead, they propose a bit-vector based compact structure, as depicted in Figure 2.2. It essentially stores only one graph $G = (V, E)$ with the same set of nodes and edges as the input uncertain graph $\mathcal{G}$. However, each edge $e$ in $G$ has a bit-vector of size $K$—its $i$-th bit represents whether the edge $e$ is present in the sampled graph $G_i$ or not.

Given an $s$-$t$ reliability query, Zhu et al. [2015] performs BFS over this compact graph structure, which is equivalent to doing BFS traversals in parallel across the pre-computed possible worlds. We attach an additional bit vector $I_v$ with each node $v$ that keeps track of the possible worlds in which $v$ is reachable from $s$. Initially, $I_s = [1\,1\,\ldots\,1]$ and $I_v = [0\,0\,\ldots\,0]$ for all $v \neq s$. Let us also denote by $U$ the set of explored vertices based on BFS. Initially, $U = \{s\}$. At each step, when we find an unexplored node $v$ that is an out-neighbor of at least one node $u$ in $U$, we insert $v$ into $U$. We update the bit vector $I_v$ to include the possible worlds where all such $v$'s are reachable from $s$. Before proceeding to the next step of BFS, one may note that

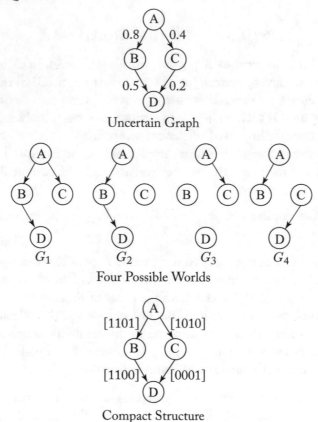

Figure 2.2: Compact data structure for multiple possible worlds.

if $v$ has some out-neighbor $w$ that is already in $U$, we may need to update $I_w$. Specifically, let $G_i$ be a possible world that is currently in $I_v$, but not in $I_w$. Then, we should also include $G_i$ in $I_w$. Such changes in $I_w$ may in turn affect $I_z$, where $z$ is an out-neighbor of $w$ and $z$ is also in $U$. In general, we proceed to the next step of BFS only after finishing these cascading updates. Finally, the number of 1's in $I_t$, divided by $K$, provides the MC sampling-based estimation of $s$-$t$ reliability.

**Recursive Sampling.** Recursive sampling, which was proposed in Jin et al. [2011b], improves on MC sampling by considering the two following factors.

- When some edges are missing in a possible world, the presence of other edges might no longer be relevant with respect to certain $s$-$t$ reliability queries. Hence, those edges can be skipped from sampling and query evaluation process.

- Many possible worlds share a significant portion of existing or missing edges. Hence, the reachability checking cost could be shared among them.

The basic approach, which follows a divide-and-conquer technique, is given below. A very similar algorithm, called the Dynamic MC sampling, was developed in Zhu et al. [2011]. We start from the source node $s$ and say that $s$ is already *reached*. An edge $e$ is *expandable* if it starts from a *reached* node. We randomly pick an extendable edge $e$, then sample the existence of $e$ for $K$ iterations. The next step is to divide the samples into two groups: one group with $e$ existing and another group with $e$ not existing. In the first group, we may reach a new vertex $w$ via $e$, and in that case, more edges become *expandable*. For both groups, we repeat the process of picking a random *expandable* edge, sampling its existence, and dividing the group into smaller batches.

Formally, let us assume that $E_1 \subseteq E$ be the set of included edges and $E_2 \subseteq E$ be the set of not-included edges in one group (referred to as a *prefix group* in Jin et al. [2011b]) at some intermediate stage of our method. Let us denote this group by $\mathcal{G}(E_1, E_2)$, i.e., the set of possible worlds of $\mathcal{G} = (V, E, p)$ which contains all edges in $E_1$, and no edges in $E_2$. Clearly, $E_1 \cup E_2 \subseteq E$ and $E_1 \cap E_2 = \phi$. The *generating probability* of the group $\mathcal{G}(E_1, E_2)$ can be defined as follows:

$$\Pr(\mathcal{G}(E_1, E_2)) = \prod_{e \in E_1} p(e) \prod_{e' \in E_2} (1 - p(e')). \tag{2.9}$$

The $s$-$t$ reliability of a group $\mathcal{G}(E_1, E_2)$ is defined as the probability that $t$ is reachable from $s$ conditioned on the existence of the group $\mathcal{G}(E_1, E_2)$, i.e.,

$$R_{\mathcal{G}(E_1, E_2)}(s, t) = \sum_{G \sqsubseteq \mathcal{G}(E_1, E_2)} I_G(s, t) \times \frac{\Pr(G)}{\Pr(\mathcal{G}(E_1, E_2))}. \tag{2.10}$$

Next, one may verify that the following holds. $R(s, t) = R_{\mathcal{G}(\phi, \phi)}(s, t)$. Also, for any edge $e \in E \setminus (E_1 \cup E_2)$,

$$R_{\mathcal{G}(E_1, E_2)}(s, t) = p(e) R_{\mathcal{G}(E_1 \cup \{e\}, E_2)}(s, t) + (1 - p(e)) R_{\mathcal{G}(E_1, E_2 \cup \{e\})}(s, t). \tag{2.11}$$

Finally, we terminate our algorithm when either $E_1$ contains an $s$-$t$ path with $R_{\mathcal{G}(E_1, E_2)}(s, t) = 1$, or $E_2$ contains an $s$-$t$ cut with $R_{\mathcal{G}(E_1, E_2)}(s, t) = 0$. The efficiency can further be improved by selecting the "best" *expendable* edge at each iteration, and Jin et al. [2011b] designed various heuristic techniques for finding such edges. This sampling process has the same variance as the basic MC sampling. The variance can be reduced by considering more sophisticated estimators, e.g., Horvitz-Thomson estimator [Jin et al., 2011b].

In the literature, various other sampling methods were also considered, e.g., Fishman [1986], Karp and Luby [1983], and Li et al. [2014], which improve the variance of basic MC sampling. Recently, lazy propagation sampling [Li et al., 2017] and probtree indexing methods [Maniu et al., 2017] have been proposed to improve the efficiency of $s$-$t$ reliability estimation.

**Indexing for Reliable Set Query.** An indexing method for the reliable set query was developed in Khan et al. [2014]. Given an uncertain graph $\mathcal{G} = (V, E, p)$, a probability threshold $\eta \in (0, 1)$, and a source node $s \in V$, the reliable set problem asks for all nodes in $V$ that are reachable from $s$ with probability greater than or equal to $\eta$. As an example, let us consider the uncertain graph in Figure 2.3. Assume that one wants to compute all nodes which are reachable from $s$ with probability greater than 0.5. It is easy to verify that $w$ is part of the solution due to a direct edge from $s$ with probability greater than the query threshold. Additionally, $u$ can be reached from $s$ directly, or via $w$. Thus, the probability that $u$ is reachable from $s$ is equal to the probability that at least one among the direct path and the path through $w$ exists. Assuming independence among the existence of the edges in the graph, this probability is: $1 - (1 - 0.5) \times (1 - 0.6 \times 0.5) = 0.65$. Hence, $u$ also belongs to the solution set. Following a similar reasoning, one may verify that the answer to our query is: $\{s, u, w\}$.

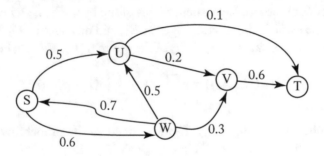

Figure 2.3: Reliability set query.

In principle, one can apply the existing reliability estimation strategies to identify the reliable set. However, for a larger threshold $\eta$, the reliability set usually consists of only the nodes in the neighborhood of the source $s$. Thus, the technique in Khan et al. [2014] limits the sampling process only inside the neighboring region of $s$, and directly prunes those nodes which are guaranteed not to be reached from $s$ with probability higher than or equal to $\eta$. For this purpose, an RQ-Tree index was proposed in Khan et al. [2014].

The RQ-Tree index is based on a hierarchical clustering of the nodes in the input uncertain graph. Specifically, the RQ-Tree, denoted as $T$, is a tree, where the root contains the complete set of nodes $V$, and the leaves correspond to individual nodes of $V$. All clusters at any level $i$ form a partition of $V$. A cluster at level $i$ is partitioned into a number of children clusters at level $i + 1$. As a result, there exists a unique path in $T$ that connects each node of $V$ to the root. Such a path is composed of clusters that are all nested into each other. An example of RQ-Tree index for the uncertain graph of Figure 2.3 is shown in Figure 2.4, together with some bounds that will be clarified below.

A key concept in the proposed index is the notion of *outreach probability*, $U_{out}(s, C)$, which is the probability that a node $s$ within a cluster $C$ in the RQ-Tree is connected to nodes outside

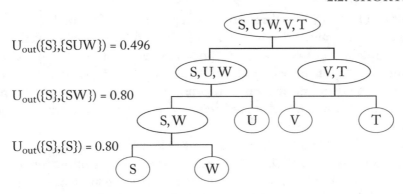

$U_{out}(\{S\},\{SUW\}) = 0.496$

$U_{out}(\{S\},\{SW\}) = 0.80$

$U_{out}(\{S\},\{S\}) = 0.80$

Figure 2.4: An RQ-Tree index for the uncertain graph in Figure 2.3.

$C$. Two interesting observations arise. (1) If the outreach probability of $s$ in $C$ is smaller than $\eta$, then the probability of reaching every node outside $C$ is also smaller than $\eta$. (2) The outreach probability values are non-decreasing for clusters that are nested into each other. The two above observations create the basis for retrieving a valid candidate set from an RQ-Tree. Specifically, one only needs to focus on the cluster $C$ having the largest outreach probability of $s$ in $C$ such that it is smaller than $\eta$. This cluster $C$ (i.e., the candidate set) can be identified by performing a bottom-up traversal in $T$, starting from the leaf node $s$.

Therefore, our query-processing strategy is based on two phases.

1. *Candidate generation*, where a candidate set of nodes is built based on the information stored into the pre-computed RQ-Tree index. All nodes not belonging to the candidate set are discarded. A nice feature of this step is to guarantee that no true positive node is discarded from the candidate set.

2. *Verification*, where an MC sampling is applied to the candidate set so to discard nodes that should not be part of the answer.

## 2.2    SHORTEST PATH

Shortest path queries over uncertain graphs consider edge weights in addition to probabilities. The problem of identifying the top-$k$ shortest paths has been studied in the literature [Yuan et al., 2010, Zou et al., 2011], which has applications in GPS enabled route planning over transportation networks. In particular, Zou et al. [2011] designed an upper- and lower-bound-based pruning algorithm to efficiently identify the top-$k$ shortest paths. As discussed in Chapter 1, the ranking of the shortest paths are based on their *shortest path probabilities*, that is, the probability that a path $P$ is indeed a shortest path in the possible worlds of the uncertain graph $\mathcal{G}$. Formally,

$$SP(P) = \sum_{G \sqsubseteq \mathcal{G}} I_{SP}(G, P) \times \Pr(G). \tag{2.12}$$

In Equation (1.2), $SP(P)$ is the shortest path probability of the path $P$. $I_{SP}(G)$ is an indicator function that takes value 1 if $P$ is a shortest path from $S$ to $T$ in the possible world $G$, and 0 otherwise. The method in Zou et al. [2011] progressively identifies the top-$k'$ shortest paths from $G$ without considering any edge probabilities, where $k' \geq k$. This can be accomplished by off-the-shelf techniques to find the top-$k'$ shortest paths in a deterministic graph, e.g., Yen's algorithm [Yen, 1971]. The exact value of $k'$ depends on the pruning criteria, which is discussed in the following.

Let us denote by $LB(P)$ and $UB(P)$ as a lower bound and an upper bound, respectively, of $SP(P)$. The algorithm [Zou et al., 2011] keeps a priority queue of the top-$k'$ shortest paths found so far based on their lower-bound $LB(.)$ values. If there are more than $k$ paths in the priority queue, and the upper bound $UB(.)$ value of the $(k'+1)$-th shortest path is smaller than than the $k$-th largest $LB(.)$ value in the priority queue, we then terminate the algorithm. This ensures that the top-$k$ shortest paths according to the shortest path probability metric must be in the set of $k'$ shortest paths inside the priority queue. One can apply Karp and Luby [1983] algorithm to efficiently identify the top-$k$ paths from this set of top-$k'$ paths.

Clearly, the efficiency of Zou et al. [2011] depends on the effectiveness of the upper and lower bounds as discussed above. Let us denote by $P_1, P_2, \ldots, P_i, \ldots, P_{k'}$ the top-$k'$ shortest paths according to Yen's algorithm. We also denote by $E(P)$ the event that the path $P$ exists in a possible world of the input uncertain graph. Then, we have the following relation:

$$
\begin{aligned}
SP(P_i) &= \Pr\left(\cap_{j=1}^{i-1}\overline{E(P_j - P_i)}\right) \cdot \Pr(E(P_i)) \\
&\geq \prod_{j=1}^{i-1}\Pr\left(\overline{E(P_j - P_i)}\right) \cdot \Pr(E(P_i)) \\
&= \prod_{j=1}^{i-1}\left(1 - \prod_{e\in(P_j-P_i)}p(e)\right) \cdot \Pr(E(P_i)) \\
&= LB_1(P_i).
\end{aligned}
\tag{2.13}
$$

The equality in the second line of Equation (2.13) holds only when the edges in $(P_j - P_i)$ are all distinct for all $j \in (1, i - 1)$. This is not often true, and therefore the above lower bound $LB_1(.)$ is not very tight. Therefore, Zou et al. [2011] developes a stricter lower bound $LB_2(.)$ by using a set cover-based approach.

Given a collection of paths $\mathcal{P}$ and a set of edges $S$, a path $P \in \mathcal{P}$ is *covered* by $S$ if and only if $P \cap S \neq \phi$, i.e., there is at least one common edge between $P$ and $S$. $S$ is a *set cover* over the path set $\mathcal{P}$ if it satisfies the following:

- for every path $P \in \mathcal{P}$, $P$ is covered by $S$; and

- $S$ cannot cover all paths in $\mathcal{P}$ if any edge $e \in S$ is removed from $S$.

Given the set of paths $(P_j - P_i)$, $j \in (1, i-1)$, let us consider the enumeration of all its set covers $S_1, S_2, \ldots, S_r$. Then, one can show that $\Pr\left(\cap_{j=1}^{n-1} \overline{E(P_j - P_i)}\right) = \Pr\left(\cup_{j=1}^{r} E\left(\overline{S_j}\right)\right)$. However, it is impossible to enumerate all set covers due to its exponential time complexity. The method in Zou et al. [2011] instead considers only the *pairwise independent* set covers $S_1', S_2', \ldots, S_{r'}'$, over the collection of paths $(P_j - P_i)$, $j \in (1, i-1)$. Two set covers are pairwise independent if there is no common edge between them. One can find the first set cover $S_1'$ by the greedy minimal set cover algorithm [Cormen et al., 2001]. Then, we remove all the edges in $S_1'$ from the collection of paths $(P_j - P_i)$, and iterate the above step until no new set cover can be found. In this way, we can find the pairwise independent set covers $S_1', S_2', \ldots, S_{r'}'$. The second lower bound can be derived as given below:

$$
\begin{aligned}
SP(P_i) &= \Pr\left(\cap_{j=1}^{i-1} \overline{E(P_j - P_i)}\right) \cdot \Pr(E(P_i)) \\
&= \Pr\left(\cup_{j=1}^{r} E\left(\overline{S_j}\right)\right) \cdot \Pr(E(P_i)) \\
&\geq \prod_{j=1}^{r'} Pr\left(E\left(\overline{S'_j}\right)\right) \cdot \Pr(E(P_i)) \\
&= LB_2(P_i).
\end{aligned}
\tag{2.14}
$$

Finally, the upper bound $UB(.)$ can be derived as follows. We omit the proof, which can be found in Zou et al. [2011]:

$$
\begin{aligned}
SP(P_i) &\leq UB(P_i) \\
&= 1 - \sum_{j=1}^{i-1} LB(P_j) \\
&= 1 - \sum_{j=1}^{i-1} \max\{LB_1(P_j), LB_2(P_j)\}.
\end{aligned}
\tag{2.15}
$$

## 2.3    NEAREST NEIGHBORS

Given a node in an uncertain graph, the nearest neighbor query asks for the top-$k$ nearest neighbors of that query node. Clearly, this involves computing the shortest path distance between two nodes. However, as discussed in Chapter 1, the semantics of the shortest path distance in an uncertain graph can vary based on applications. Potamias et al. [2010] proposes a series of shortest path distances over uncertain graphs, e.g., median distance, majority distance, and expected-reliable distance, as defined below.

**Shortest Path Distribution.** We define the distribution $\mathbf{p}_{s,t}(d)$ of shortest path distance $d$ between $s$ and $t$ as:

$$
\mathbf{p}_{s,t}(d) = \sum_{G | d_G(s,t) = d} \Pr(G).
\tag{2.16}
$$

In other words, $\mathbf{p}_{s,t}(d)$ adds up the probabilities of all possible worlds in which the shortest path distance from $s$ to $t$ is exactly $d$.

**Median Distance.** The median distance $d_M(s,t)$ is the median of the shortest path distance distribution $\mathbf{p}_{s,t}(d)$ considering all possible worlds. Formally,

$$d_M(s,t) = \underset{D}{argmax} \left\{ \sum_{d=0}^{D} \mathbf{p}_{s,t}(d) \leq \frac{1}{2} \right\}. \tag{2.17}$$

**Majority Distance.** The majority distance $d_J(s,t)$ is defined as the most probable shortest path distance, i.e.,

$$d_J(s,t) = \underset{d}{argmax} \left\{ \mathbf{p}_{s,t}(d) \right\}. \tag{2.18}$$

One may note that both the median and majority distances can be infinite. We define below the expected-reliable distance which eliminates this problem by disregarding the possible worlds where no path exists from $s$ to $t$.

**Expected-Reliable Distance.** The expected-reliable distance is defined as the expected shortest path distance in all possible worlds in which there exists a path from $s$ to $t$. Formally,

$$d_{ER}(s,t) = \sum_{d \mid d < \infty} d \cdot \frac{\mathbf{p}_{s,t}(d)}{1 - \mathbf{p}_{s,t}(\infty)}. \tag{2.19}$$

Based on the aforementioned definitions, we can find the top-$k$ nearest neighbors for a given query node. A baseline approach will compute the shortest path distance from $s$ to every other node in the uncertain graph, and then will report the top-$k$ ones. However, for small values of $k$, it could be be an wastage of computation. Therefore, the challenge lies in efficiently finding the nearest neighbors without computing the shortest path distances for all other nodes. In this context, we shall discuss the pruning algorithm designed in Potamias et al. [2010] to identify the top-$k$ nearest neighbors based on median distance.

Potamias et al. [2010] introduces the notion of shortest path distance distribution truncated to smaller distances. In particular, for a distance smaller than $D$, the new distribution $\mathbf{p}_{D,s,t}(d)$ is identical to $\mathbf{p}_{s,t}(d)$. The remaining probability mass is concentrated at distance $D$. Formally,

$$\mathbf{p}_{D,s,t}(d) = \begin{cases} \mathbf{p}_{s,t}(d), & \text{if } d < D \\ \sum_{x=D}^{\infty} \mathbf{p}_{s,t}(x), & \text{if } d = D \\ 0, & \text{if } d > D. \end{cases}$$

Let us denote by $d_{D,M}(s,t)$ the median distance obtained from the distribution $\mathbf{p}_{D,s,t}$, and $d_M(s,t)$ be the actual median distance that we would have obtained from the real distribution $\mathbf{p}_{s,t}$. One can verify that for any two nodes $t_1, t_2 \in V$, if $d_{D,M}(s,t_1) < d_{D,M}(s,t_2)$, then it implies $d_M(s,t_1) < d_M(s,t_2)$. A direct corollary of the above observation is that if we find the set of

$k$ nodes $T_k(s) = \{t_1, t_2, \ldots, t_k\}$ for which $d_{D,M}(s, t_i) < d_{D,M}(s, t)$, for all $t_i \in T_k(s)$ and $t \in V \setminus T_k(s)$, we can declare the set $T_k(s)$ to be the answer to the top-$k$ nearest neighbor query. The pruning scheme in Potamias et al. [2010] is based on the above idea.

In particular, we initially set a small value for $D$, and perform Dijkstra's algorithm up to distance $D$ from the query node $s$, by simultaneously generating $K$ MC samples. This helps us to compute $\mathbf{p}_{D,s,t}$ for all $t \in V$ that have been visited at least once from $s$ in the above process. Among these nodes, we select the ones for which $d_{D,M}(s, t) < D$, and insert them into a list $T_k(s)$. If $T_k$ has size at least $k$, we found the top-$k$ nearest neighbors of $s$. Otherwise, we repeat the above process with larger $D$.

## SUMMARY

In this chapter we introduced reliability, shortest path, and nearest neighbor queries over uncertain graphs. We briefly discussed their complexity, as well as various sampling, indexing, and pruning techniques to efficiently answer them.

CHAPTER 3

# Graph Pattern Matching Queries

A significant amount of research has been devoted to seeking efficient solutions to the problem of pattern matching over graphs. This interest is largely due to the many applications that require such efficient solutions, including protein complex prediction, social network analysis, and structural pattern recognition. However, in many real applications, the graph data are often noisy, incomplete, and inaccurate. In other words, there exist many uncertain graphs. Therefore, in this chapter, we study pattern matching in the context of large uncertain graphs. Specifically, we want to retrieve all qualified matches of a query pattern in the uncertain graph. Though pattern matching over uncertain graphs is NP-hard, we employ a *filtering-and-verification* framework to speed up the search. In the filtering phase, we propose a *probabilistic matching tree* (PM-tree) built from match cuts obtained by a cut selection process. Based on the PM-tree, we devise a *collective pruning* strategy to prune a large number of unqualified matches. During the verification phase, we develop an efficient sampling algorithm to validate the remaining candidates.

## 3.1 THE PATTERN MATCHING PROBLEM

In this section, we define some necessary concepts and discuss the complexity of the graph matching problem.

**Uncertain Graph.** An undirected deterministic graph $g^c$ is denoted by $(V, E, \Sigma, L)$, where $V$ is a set of vertices, $E$ is a set of edges ($\subseteq V \times V$), $\Sigma$ is a set of labels, and $L : V \to \Sigma$ is a function that assigns labels to vertices. An uncertain graph is defined as $g = (g^c, \mathrm{Pr})$, where $\mathrm{Pr} : E \to (0, 1]$ is a function that assigns existence probabilities to edges in $E$.

**Possible World Graph.** A possible world graph $g' = (V', E', \Sigma', L')$ is an instantiation of an uncertain graph $g = ((V, E, \Sigma, L), \mathrm{Pr})$, where $V' = V$, $E' \subseteq E$, and $\Sigma' = \Sigma$. We denote the relationship between $g'$ and $g$ by $g \Rightarrow g'$. We use $PWG(g)$ to denote the set of all possible world graphs derived from $g$.

Following the convention in Jin et al. [2011b], Potamias et al. [2010], Yuan et al. [2012, 2015], Zou et al. [2010a,c], we assume that the existence of different edges in an uncertain graph are independent. Then, the probability of a possible world graph $g'$ is given by:

$$\mathrm{Pr}(g \Rightarrow g') = \prod_{e \in E'} \mathrm{Pr}(e) \prod_{e \in E \setminus E'} (1 - \mathrm{Pr}(e)). \tag{3.1}$$

**Match** [Fan et al., 2011, Zou et al., 2009a]. Consider a deterministic graph $g^c$, a connected graph pattern query $q$ that has $n$ vertices $\{v_1, ..., v_n\}$, and a shortest path threshold $\gamma$. A set of $n$ distinct vertices $m = \{u_1, ..., u_n\}$ in $g^c$ is said to be a match for $q$, denoted by $m \trianglerighteq_q g^c$, if and only if the following conditions hold: (1) $L(u_i) = L(v_i)\ \forall i \in [1,n]$, where $L(u_i)$ denotes the label of $u_i$; and (2) If there is an edge between $v_i$ and $v_j$ in $q$, the shortest-path distance between $u_i$ and $u_j$ in $g^c$ is no larger than $\gamma$.

For example, in Figure 3.1, assume that all edge weights of $ug^c$ are 1 and $\gamma = 3$. Then, the vertex set $\{5, 6, 7\}$ is a match for $q$ in $ug^c$. Vertex set $\{1, 5, 7\}$ is not a match for $q$ in $ug^c$ because the distance between vertices 1 and 7 is larger than $\gamma$.

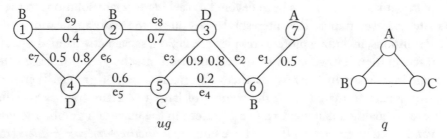

Figure 3.1: Uncertain graph $ug$ and query pattern $q$.

**Pattern Matching Probability.** For a graph pattern query $q$, an uncertain graph $g$ and a vertex set $m$ in $g$, we define the pattern matching probability of $m$ in $g$ under $q$ as:

$$\Pr(m \trianglerighteq_q g) = \sum_{g' \in PM(q,g)} \Pr(g \Rightarrow g'), \qquad (3.2)$$

where $PM(q, g)$ is $g$'s possible world graphs that contain $m$ as a match for $q$, that is, $PM(q, g) = \{g' | m \trianglerighteq_q g', g' \in PWG(g)\}$.

Note that, if $m$ is a match for $q$ in the possible world graph $g'$, then $m$ must satisfy the associated conditions: (1) the vertex labels of $m$ are the same as the corresponding vertex labels of $q$; and (2) each pair of vertices of $m$ in $g'$ has shortest-path distance within the threshold $\gamma$.

**Probabilistic Pattern Matching.** Given an uncertain graph $g$, a graph pattern query $q$, and a probability threshold $\epsilon$ $(0 < \epsilon \le 1)$, a pattern matching query returns all vertex sets in $g$, $\{m | \Pr(m \trianglerighteq_q g) \ge \epsilon, m \subseteq V(g)\}$.

Thus, in order to answer probabilistic pattern matching queries efficiently, we must be able to calculate PMP (the pattern matching probability) efficiently. We now show the complexity of calculating PMP.

**Theorem 3.1**  *Computing pattern matching probability is NP-hard.*

**Proof.** We reduce the well-known NP-complete problem STEINER Tree [Garey and Johnson, 1979] to computing the pattern matching probability. Consider a graph pattern query

$q$ and a vertex set $m$ that has been found to be a valid match for $g^c$. We must determine whether $m$ is also a valid match for $g$, i.e., whether the PMP of $m$ in $g$ is at least a given threshold. Assume the existence probability of each edge in $g$ is equal to $p$. Define a pathset as a set of edges that connect the vertices in $m$. Based on the definition of PMP, we easily obtain the PMP as:

$$\Pr(m \trianglerighteq_q g) = \sum_{i=1}^{|E|} N_i\, p^i\, (1-p)^{|E|-i}, \tag{3.3}$$

where $N_i$ is the number of $i$-edge pathsets that connect all the vertices in $m$ and $|E|$ is the number of edges of $g$.

An instance of STEINER TREE is a graph $g^c = (V, E)$, a set $m$ of target vertices, and an integer bound $b$. One has to determine whether there is a Steiner tree with $b$ or fewer edges in $g^c$; that is, one must decide whether there is a set of $b$ or fewer edges which connect all of the target vertices in $m$ by paths. Using an algorithm calculating $\Pr(m \trianglerighteq_q g)$, we produce the sequence of pathset numbers $N_1, ..., N_{|E|}$ in Equation (3.3). We then extract $l$, the size of a minimum pathset. Since $l$ is the index of the first non-zero term in the pathset numbers, it is easily extracted. A pathset for $g^c$ and $m$ contains at least a Steiner tree for $m$; hence, the minimum pathset is a minimum Steiner tree. Thus, we just check whether $l \leq b$, which completes the reduction.

## 3.2   FILTERING-AND-VERIFICATION FRAMEWORK

Figure 3.2 gives a high-level overview of our general framework for a pattern matching query $q$ over an uncertain graph $g$. It consists of three phases, namely *Structural pruning*, *Probabilistic pruning*, and *Verification*. The first two phases belong to the filtering step, and the last one is the verification step. We briefly present each step in what follows.

> **Procedure** PatternMatch_Framework {
>     **Input:** a graph pattern query $q$, an uncertain graph $g$, a threshold $\epsilon$
>     **Output:** matches whose pattern matching probabilities are at least $\epsilon$
>     (1)  perform structeural pruning     *//struct. prune phase*
>     (2)  perform probabilistic pruning   *//prob. prune phase*
>     (3)  perform verification            *//verification phase*
> }

Figure 3.2: Framework for pattern matching on an uncertain graph.

**Structural Pruning.** The idea of structural pruning is straightforward. For $n$ vertices $m = \{u_1, ..., u_n\}$ in $g$, if we remove all of the uncertainty in the uncertain graph $g$, and $m$ is still not a match for $q$ in the resulting graph, then $m$ cannot be a match for $q$ in the original uncertain graph.

Formally, for $m = \{u_1, ..., u_n\} \in g$, let $g^c$ denote the *corresponding deterministic graph* after we remove all the uncertain information from $g$. Then, the following must hold.

**Theorem 3.2**   *If $m \not\trianglerighteq_q g^c$, $\Pr(m \trianglerighteq_q g) = 0$.*

**Proof.** If $m \not\trianglerighteq_q g^c$, then either (1) $m$ and $q$ do not have the same vertex labels, or (2) the distance of one pair of vertices in $m$ is larger than the distance threshold $\gamma$. If condition in (1) is met, then it is clear that $\Pr(m \trianglerighteq_q g) = 0$. Let us consider condition (2). Without loss of generality, assume that the distance of the corresponding pair of vertices is $d_1 > \gamma$. In any possible world $g'$ of $g$, let the distance of that pair of vertices be $d_2$. Since $g'$ has fewer than or the same number of edges as $g^c$, we have $d_2 \geq d_1 > \gamma$. In this case, $m \not\trianglerighteq_q g'$, that is, $m$ is not a match in any possible world of $g$. It follows that $\Pr(m \trianglerighteq_q g) = 0$.

Theorem 3.2 shows that only qualified matches in $g^c$ under $q$ can be candidates of the T-PM query. Based on this observation, given $g$ and $q$, we can obtain candidate matches using conventional deterministic graph pattern matching methods. In this chapter, we adopt the method in Zou et al. [2009a] to quickly compute a preliminary set of candidates. That method uses a distanced-based joining algorithm and many pruning strategies to greatly reduce the search space without performing pairwise matching computation, which enables higher running efficiency than other known graph pattern matching algorithms [Fan et al., 2011]. Assume that the result is $SC_q = \{m | m \trianglerighteq_q g^c\}$, then $SC_q$ becomes the input for uncertain pattern matching in the next step of our approach.

**Probabilistic Pruning.** In this step, we propose a tight upper bound, *UpperB*, for the pattern matching probability, i.e., $\Pr(m \trianglerighteq_q g) \leq UpperB$. For the given threshold $\epsilon$, if $UpperB < \epsilon$, $m$ can be pruned safely. In this step, we propose one-by-one and collective pruning algorithms to efficiently obtain the candidate set $C_q$ that eventually becomes the input of the final verification step.

**Verification.** In this step, we calculate the true $\Pr(m \trianglerighteq_q g)$ for each remaining candidate answer $m$ in $C_q$, to ensure that $m$ is a true answer, i.e., $\Pr(m \trianglerighteq_q g) \geq \epsilon$.

## 3.3   PROBABILISTIC PRUNING

As mentioned above, we first conduct structural pruning to obtain a set of qualified candidate matches of $q$ in $g$. We then use probabilistic pruning techniques to further filter the remaining match set, $SC_q$.

The idea behind probabilistic pruning is to compute and use an upper bound for PMP. To facilitate this process, we propose an indexing structure, called *Probabilistic Matching Tree* (PM-tree).

Before we describe the structure of PM-trees, we begin with some definitions. Given a deterministic graph $g^c$, a *cut* in $g^c$ is a partitioning of $V(g^c)$ into two disjoint sets $(X, \overline{X})$, where $X, \overline{X} \subseteq V(g^c)$, $X \cup \overline{X} = V(g^c)$. Any edge $(u, v) \in E(g^c)$ with $u \in X$ and $v \in \overline{X}$ is said to be *crossing* the cut, and is called a *cut edge*. The set of all cut edges of $(X, \overline{X})$ is denoted by $\delta(X)$. An $x$-$y$ cut is a split of the vertices $V(g^c)$ into two disjoint sets $X$ and $\overline{X}$, such that $x \in X$ and $y \in \overline{X}$.

For example, in Figure 3.1, $(X = \{1, 2, 4\}, \overline{X} = \{3, 5, 6, 7\})$ is a cut in the graph $ug^c$, and $\{e_5, e_8\}$ are cut edges of $(X, \overline{X})$. $(X, \overline{X})$ is a 1-6 cut since $1 \in \{1, 2, 4\}$ and $6 \in \{3, 5, 6, 7\}$.

**Definition 3.3   (Probabilistic Matching Tree)** A PM-tree is a tree $T = (V(T), E(T))$. Each node of $T$ is a vertex of $V(g^c)$, i.e., $V(T) = V(g^c)$. Each edge $e \in E(T)$ of $T$ satisfies the following property: for each pair of distinct nodes $(s, t)$ and an edge $e$ on the unique path between $s$ and $t$, deleting $e$ separates $T$ into two connected components, $X$ and $\overline{X}$. Under these conditions, $(X, \overline{X})$ is an $s$-$t$ cut in $g^c$. Specifically, deleting $e = (u, v) \in E(T)$ results in a $u$-$v$ cut for $u \in U$ and $v \in \overline{U}$. We attach all cut edges of the $u$-$v$ cut to edge $e$. We also calculate the connected probability between $U$ and $\overline{U}$, and associate its value to $e$.

Note that, to avoid confusion, we use *node* for $T$, and *vertex* for uncertain graph $g$.

**Example 3.4**   Figure 3.3 shows the PM-tree of the graph $ug$ of Figure 3.1. PM-tree is clearly a tree structure $T$. Deleting edge $(4, 3)$ divides $T$ into two parts $(X = \{1, 2, 4\}, \overline{X} = \{3, 5, 6, 7\})$, which is a cut in $ug^c$. The cut edge set $\delta(X) = \{e_5, e_8\}$ and its connected probability 0.88 are indexed by the edge $(4, 3)$.

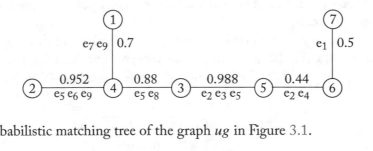

Figure 3.3: Probabilistic matching tree of the graph $ug$ in Figure 3.1.

Let $\delta(U) = \{e_1, ..., e_{|\delta(U)|}\}$ denote the set of all cut edges between $U$ and $\overline{U}$. Then the connected probability between $U$ and $\overline{U}$ is calculated as follows:

$$\Pr(U, \overline{U}) = 1 - \prod_{i=1}^{|\delta(U)|} [1 - \Pr(e_i)]. \qquad (3.4)$$

Furthermore, we need to define *match cuts*. For $m = \{u_1, ..., u_n\} \in SC_q$, a match cut of $m$ is a set of edges in $g^c$ whose removal causes some vertices of $\{u_1, ..., u_n\}$ in $g^c$ to become disconnected.

For example, consider $m = \{2, 5, 7\}$ in the deterministic graph $ug^c$ shown in Figure 3.1. The edge set $\{e_2, e_4\}$ or $\{e_1\}$ is a match cut of $m$, since the removal of either of them separates 7 and $\{2, 5\}$.

Let $Mc = \{c_1, .., c_{|Mc|}\}$ be the set of all match cuts of $m$ in the deterministic graph $g^c$, $Bc_i$ be Boolean variables for $1 \leq i \leq |Mc|$, and $\Pr(Bc_i)$ be the probability of the match cut $c_i$ existing in $g$, then the following lemma gives a bound on the pattern match probability.

**Lemma 3.5**

$$\Pr(m \trianglerighteq_q g) \leq 1 - \Pr(Bc_1 \vee ... \vee Bc_{|Mc|})$$
$$= \Pr(\overline{Bc_1} \wedge ... \wedge \overline{Bc_{|Mc|}}). \tag{3.5}$$

**Proof.** We provide a rough sketch of the proof. We consider the probability of $m$ not being a match in $g$, which is given by $1 - \Pr(m \trianglerighteq_q g)$. First, we group possible worlds into different groups such that a possible world in the $i$th group does not contain a match where each pair of vertices has distance at most $i$ hops ($i \leq \gamma$). We then delete edges in possible world graphs in each group until each graph corresponds to a set of match cuts. We also exchange possible world graphs from different groups until graphs in each new group have the same number of match cuts. Finally, we use the *Inclusion-Exclusion Principle* to derive the conclusion.

*Remark.* The match in Lemma 3.5 is a remaining match after structural pruning.

To compute the upper bound, we should unfold the Equation (3.5). However, such unfolding requires an exponential number of steps. Hence, to compute an upper bound efficiently, we adopt the following strategy.

If we select a group of match cuts, $IN = \{c_1, ..., c_{|IN|}\}$, that are disjoint in $g^c$, the corresponding Boolean variables $\{Bc_1, ..., Bc_{|IN|}\}$ are independent of each other as well. Since $IN \subseteq Mc$, then $\wedge_{i=1}^{|IN|} \overline{Bc_i} \supseteq \wedge_{j=1}^{|Mc|} \overline{Bc_j}$ holds, and an upper bound for $\Pr(m \trianglerighteq_q g)$ is obtained as follows:

$$\Pr(m \trianglerighteq_q g) \leq \Pr(\overline{Bc_1} \wedge ... \wedge \overline{Bc_{|Mc|}})$$
$$\leq \Pr(\overline{Bc_1} \wedge ... \wedge \overline{Bc_{|IN|}})$$
$$= \prod_{i=1}^{|IN|} [\Pr(\overline{Bc_i})] \tag{3.6}$$
$$= UpperB.$$

**Pruning Algorithm:** Recall that a PM-tree is a tree structure $T$, and any edge on the unique path between a pair of nodes $s$ and $t$, indexes a set of cut edges $\delta(U)$ between $s$ and $t$ in $g^c$. Based on the definition of a match cut, the cut edge set $\delta(U)$ is a match cut for any $m = \{u_1, ...u_n\}$ containing $s$ and $t$. To conduct probabilistic pruning, we first locate each corresponding node in $T$ for $m = \{u_1, ...u_n\}$. We traverse all edges in $T$ that connect the nodes in $m$, and obtain both their indexed cut edges and the corresponding probabilities as given by Equation (3.4). This can be done using breadth-first search in $T$ starting in any node contained in $m$, stopping when all nodes in $m$ have been encountered. Next we choose a group of disjoint match cuts and obtain an upper bound using Equation (3.6). If the upper bound is smaller than the threshold $\epsilon$, the candidate $m$ is pruned. We denote the probabilistic pruning condition by $CND \triangleq UpperB < \epsilon$. In $T$, $\Pr(\overline{Bc_i})$ is the probability of cut edges disappearing, which is given by Equation (3.4). Thus, Equation (3.6) can now be rewritten as

$$
\begin{aligned}
\Pr(m \trianglerighteq_q g) &\leq \prod_{i=1}^{|IN|} [\Pr(\overline{Bc_i})] \\
&= \prod_{i=1}^{|IN|} [1 - \prod_{e \in c_i} (1 - \Pr(e))] \\
&= UpperB.
\end{aligned}
\tag{3.7}
$$

Note that we have calculated $\Pr(\overline{Bc_i})$ offline and attached the value to the corresponding edge in the PM-tree.

In all match cuts obtained from the PM-tree, there are many groups of disjoint match cuts, which leads to different upper bounds. We want the bound to be as tight as possible to increase the pruning power. We transform the problem of computing tightest $UpperB$ into the set packing problem.

**Tightest** $UpperB$. For a match, given the set of all match cuts $S = \{c_1, .., c_i, .., c_{|S|}\}$, obtained from the PM-tree, with each $c_i$ having a weight given by $-\ln(\Pr(\overline{Bc_i}))$, we want a collection of disjoint match cuts $S' \subseteq S$ that maximizes $\sum_{c_i \in S'} -\ln(\Pr(\overline{Bc_i}))$.

Let $v = \sum_{c_i \in S'} -\ln(\Pr(\overline{Bc_i}))$. Based on Equation (3.6), $UpperB = e^{-v}$. Thus, maximizing $v$ means minimizing $UpperB$, and we can obtain the tightest (smallest) $UpperB$. It is well known that set packing is NP-hard [Garey and Johnson, 1979]. In Balas and Xue [1996], the maximum-weight set packing problem is formulated as a 0–1 integer programming problem. The integer programming programming is relaxed to be a linear programming that returns a very tight approximation, $z$, on the weight of the maximum packing set, and there is an efficient algorithm that can solve this linear programming problem. Therefore, we use $e^{-z}$ computed by the solution given in Balas and Xue [1996] as the upper bound for $\Pr(m \trianglerighteq_q g)$.

## 3.4 VERIFICATION

In this section, we compute the pattern matching probability (PMP) of a match in $C_q$ to determine the final answer set. Specifically, given the hardness of computing PMP, we propose sampling algorithms to estimate PMP.

## 3.4.1   BASIC SAMPLING

In this subsection, we present a basic sampling algorithm based on Monte Carlo theory.

During the sampling process, we sample $N$ *possible world graphs*, $g_1, g_2, \ldots, g_N$, according to the existence probability of each edge in $g$. For each such sampled possible world graph $g_i$, we check whether a candidate match $m = \{u_1, \ldots, u_n\}$ is valid in $g_i$. We set a flag $y_i$ for each $g_i$, such that

$$y_i = \begin{cases} 1 & \text{if } m \text{ is a valid match in } g_i \\ 0 & \text{otherwise.} \end{cases}$$

Thus, the estimator $\widehat{\theta}_B$ is equal to

$$\widehat{\theta}_B = \widehat{\Pr(m \trianglerighteq_q g)} = \frac{\sum_{i=1}^{N} y_i}{N}. \tag{3.8}$$

For any sampling method, the *Mean Square Error (MSE)* incorporates both bias and precision of an estimator $\widehat{\theta}_B$ into a measure of overall accuracy. It is given by

$$MSE(\widehat{\theta}_B) = E[(\widehat{\theta}_B - \theta)^2] = Var(\widehat{\theta}_B) + Bias(\widehat{\theta}_B, \theta).$$

The bias of an estimator is defined as

$$Bias(\widehat{\theta}_B) = E(\widehat{\theta}_B) - \theta.$$

An estimator of $\theta$ is unbiased if its bias is 0 for all values of $\theta$, that is, $E(\widehat{\theta}_B) = \theta$. Since the estimator of the Monte Carlo method is unbiased [Fishman, 1991], it follows that

$$MSE(\widehat{\theta}_B) = Var(\widehat{\theta}_B) = \frac{1}{N}\theta(1-\theta) \approx \frac{1}{N}\widehat{\theta}_B(1-\widehat{\theta}_B), \tag{3.9}$$

where $\theta = \Pr(m \trianglerighteq_q g)$.

## 3.4.2   TREE-BASED SAMPLING

In this subsection, we introduce a tree-based sampling algorithm. To facilitate our discussion, we first introduce the notion of a $\gamma$-path set. A $\gamma$-path set $f$ connects each pair of vertices of a match $m = \{u_1, \ldots, u_n\}$ within distance $\gamma$. Specifically, any vertex-pair path in $f$ has length less than or equal to distance constraint $\gamma$. In fact, $f$ contains a Steiner tree. This Steiner tree is such that its leaves are $\{u_1, \ldots, u_n\}$, and it has the fewest edges connecting $\{u_1, \ldots, u_n\}$ within distance $\gamma$. Thus, without loss of generality, we assume that $f$ is such a Steiner tree for vertices in $\{u_1, \ldots, u_n\}$. Computing a Steiner tree is NP-complete, so we use the efficient approximation algorithm described in [ed.] to obtain all Steiner trees for $m$.

Based on the *Inclusion–Exclusion Principle*, we obtain

$$\Pr(m \trianglerighteq_q g) = \Pr\left(Bf_1 \vee \ldots \vee Bf_{|F|}\right), \tag{3.10}$$

where $Bf$ is a Boolean variable for $f$, and $\Pr(Bf)$ is the probability of $f$ in $g$. Equation (3.10) can be simplified to

$$\Pr(m \trianglerighteq_q g) = \sum_{i=1}^{|F|} (-1)^i \sum_{J \subseteq \{1,...,|F|\},|J|=i} \Pr\left(\wedge_{j=1}^{|J|} Bf_j\right). \tag{3.11}$$

Clearly, an exponential number of steps is needed for the exact calculation. Hence, we develop a sampling algorithm to estimate $\Pr(m \trianglerighteq_q g)$.

Assume Steiner trees in $F$ have total edges $\{e_1,...,e_k\}$ and $Be$ is the Boolean variable corresponding to $e$. Then each $Bf$ can be written in the form of a conjunction of some of the $Be$'s.

Based on Monte Carlo theory, the value of adopted for the number of samples, namely $N = (4 \ln 2/\xi)/\tau^2$, guarantees the estimated quality [Mitzenmacher and Upfal, 2005].

**Lemma 3.6**    *For any $\xi$ $(0 < \xi < 1)$ and $\tau$ $(\tau > 0)$, if $N \geq (4 \ln \frac{2}{\xi})/\tau^2$ then,*

$$\Pr[|Cnt/N - \Pr(m \trianglerighteq_q g)| < \xi \Pr(m \trianglerighteq_q g)] \geq 1 - \tau.$$

In Monte Carlo theory, the values of $\xi$ and $\tau$ are usually both set to 0.1 [Jin et al., 2011b, Mitzenmacher and Upfal, 2005]. The tree-based estimator is unbiased and has the following variance:

$$Var\left(\widehat{\theta}_T\right) = \frac{1}{N}\left(\sum_{i=1}^{|F|} \Pr(Bf_i) - \theta\right), \tag{3.12}$$

where $\theta = \Pr(m \trianglerighteq_q g)$.

Thus, depending on whether $\sum_{i=1}^{|F|} \Pr(Bf_i)$ is larger than or less than 1, the variance of $\widehat{\theta}_T$ can be larger or smaller than that of $\widehat{\theta}_B$.

The key issue in this approach is the repeated computations for the large number of Steiner trees within $\{u_1,...,u_n\}$. The reason is that we must first enumerate all Steiner trees within $\{u_1,...,u_n\}$, then sample these trees again. In the sampling, we also need to store all these trees to guarantee the correct sampling. This can be expensive in terms of both computational and memory costs.

## 3.4.3    HYBRID SAMPLING

The basic sampling algorithm is not suitable for large-scale uncertain graphs and high accuracy requirements, since a high accuracy requirement leads to a large number of samples that must each sample be subjected to deterministic pattern matching. The tree-based sampling algorithm must enumerate and maintain a large number of Steiner trees, thus it also needs a large number of samples. To overcome these limitations, we propose an efficient approximation algorithm, based on *Unequal Probability Sampling*, to estimate PMP. The basic idea is to group samples together to avoid exponential growth and reduce the number of pattern matching tests.

Our proposed sampling algorithm is a hybrid approach based on both *Steiner trees* and *match cuts*. Hybrid sampling introduces an early stopping strategy, that can divide all possible graphs into several groups and stop each sampling process as early as possible, as per the following theorem.

**Theorem 3.7**    *Given an uncertain graph g, a query q, the set of Steiner trees, the set of match cuts, and the current sampled graph $g_i$, hybrid sampling can be stopped whenever either one of the following conditions is satisfied: (1) $g_i$ must have a valid match if $g_i$ contains a Steiner tree, or (2) $g_i$ does not have any valid match if $g_i$ contains a match cut.*

Since we only want to know which possible graphs have a valid match or do not have any valid match, it is not necessary to sample each possible world graph exactly. Instead, we end each sampling as early as possible, as long as the valid (or invalid) condition is known. The early stopping strategy speeds up each sampling. As we also wish to reduce the size of the sampling space, we employ an unbiased unequal-probability sampling estimator, the Horvitz-Thompson estimator [Thompson, 2012], which cannot only depend on the distinct samples but also provide a smaller variance than that of the basic sampling estimator. In other words, the duplicate samples are not considered. Thus, the sampling space of the hybrid approach is significantly smaller than that of basic sampling and tree-based sampling.

**Definition 3.8**    (Horvitz-Thompson Estimator [Thompson, 2012]) Given an uncertain graph $g$, a query graph $q$, the number of samples $N$, the weight of each sample based on the early stopping strategy $w_i$ $(1 \leq i \leq n)$, the Horvitz-Thompson estimator is

$$\widehat{\theta}_{HT} = \sum_{i=1}^{v} \frac{w_i}{\pi_i},$$

where $\theta = \Pr(m \unrhd_q g)$, $\pi_i = 1 - (1 - q_i)^N$, $q_i$ is the sampled probability, and $v$ is the number of distinct sampled graphs.

Based on the early stopping strategy and the Horvitz-Thompson estimator, we design an efficient hybrid sampling algorithm.

In sampling an instance of $g$, we check if one of the early stopping conditions is satisfied. When the current sample has a valid match (early stopping condition 1), we stop the current sampling and calculate the parameters $w_i$ and $\pi_i$ of the Horvitz-Thompson estimator. When the current sample does not have any valid match (early stopping condition 2), we stop the current sampling and assign 0 to the Horvitz-Thompson estimator. Finally, we can obtain the estimator of PMP, i.e., $\widehat{\theta}_{HT}$. Note that $Var(\widehat{\theta}_{HT}) \leq \text{Min}\{Var(\widehat{\theta}_B), Var(\widehat{\theta}_T)\}$. Hence, the hybrid sampling algorithm is more efficient and reaches a more accurate estimator than either the basic or tree-based sampling algorithms.

## SUMMARY

Uncertain graphs are pervasive in many real-world applications, such as social network, where data often exhibit uncertainties. In this chapter, we study the problem of retrieving matches from large uncertain graphs that satisfy a query graph pattern with high confidence. To efficiently tackle this problem, we propose a tree index structure to enable an adaptive pruning process, designed according to a formal cost model, so that the index not only has a small size but also has powerful pruning capability. Based on the index, several pruning techniques are developed, such as best upper bounds and collective pruning, to significantly reduce the search space.

CHAPTER 4

# Graph Similarity Search Queries

Many studies have been conducted on seeking an efficient solution for graph similarity search over certain (deterministic) graphs due to its wide application in many fields, including bioinformatics, social network analysis, and Resource Description Framework (RDF) data management. However, in reality, graphs are often noisy and uncertain due to various factors, such as errors in data extraction, inconsistencies in data integration, and for privacy preserving purposes. Therefore, in this chapter, we study similarity graph containment search on large uncertain graph databases. Similarity graph containment search consists of subgraph similarity search and supergraph similarity search. Different from previous works assuming that edges in an uncertain graph arc independent of each other, we study uncertain graphs where edges' occurrences are correlated. Though subgraph or supergraph similarity search over uncertain graphs is NP-hard, we employ a *filter-and-verify* framework to speed up these two queries. For the subgraph similarity query, in the *filtering* phase, we develop tight lower and upper bounds of *subgraph similarity probability* based on a *Probabilistic Matrix Index* (PMI). During the *verification* phase, we develop an efficient sampling algorithm to validate the remaining candidates. For the supergraph similarity query, in the *filtering* phase, we propose two pruning algorithms, one light-weight and the other strong, based on *maximal common subgraphs* of query graph and data graph. In the *verification*, we design an approximate algorithm based on the *Horvitz-Thompson* estimator to fast validate the remaining candidates.

## 4.1 THE SIMILARITY SEARCH PROBLEM

In this section, we define some necessary concepts and show the complexity of our problem.

**Deterministic Graph.** An undirected deterministic graph[1] $g^c$, is denoted as $(V, E, \Sigma, L)$, where $V$ is a set of vertices, $E$ is a set of edges, $\Sigma$ is a set of labels, and $L : V \cup E \to \Sigma$ is a function that assigns labels to vertices and edges. A set of edges are *neighbor edges*, denoted by *ne*, if they are incident to the same vertex or the edges form a triangle in $g^c$.

For example, consider graph 001 in Figure 4.1. Edges $e_1$, $e_2$, and $e_3$ are neighbor edges, since they form a triangle. Consider graph 002 in Figure 4.1. Edges $e_3$, $e_4$, and $e_5$ are also neighbor edges, since they are incident to the same vertex.

---

[1]In this chapter, we consider undirected graphs, although it is straightforward to extend our methods to directed graphs.

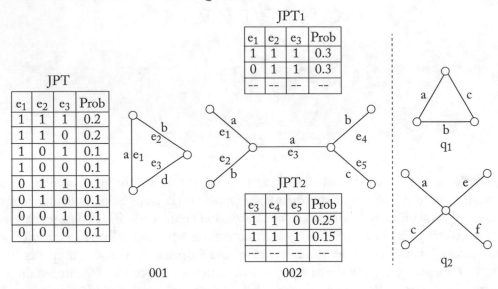

Figure 4.1: Uncertain graph database and query graph.

**Uncertain Graph.** An undirected deterministic graph $g^c$ is denoted by $(V, E, \Sigma, L)$, where $V$ is a set of vertices, $E$ is a set of edges ($\subseteq V \times V$), $\Sigma$ is a set of labels, and $L : V \to \Sigma$ is a function that assigns labels to vertices. An uncertain graph is defined as $g = (g^c, \Pr)$, where $\Pr : E \to (0, 1]$ is a function that assigns existence probabilities to edges in $E$.

**Possible World Graph.** A possible world graph $g' = (V', E', \Sigma', L')$ is an instantiation of an uncertain graph $g = ((V, E, \Sigma, L), X_E)$, where $V' = V$, $E' \subseteq E$, $\Sigma' \subseteq \Sigma$. We denote the instantiation from $g$ to $g'$ as $g \Rightarrow g'$.

**Conditional Independence.** Let $X$, $Y$, and $Z$ be sets of random variables. $X$ is conditionally independent of $Y$ given $Z$ (denoted by $X \perp Y | Z$) in distribution $\Pr$ if:

$$\Pr(X = x; Y = y | Z = z) = \Pr(X = x | Z = z)$$
$$\Pr(Y = y | Z = z),$$

for all values $x \in dom(X)$, $y \in dom(Y)$, and $z \in dom(Z)$.

Following real applications [Chui et al., 2007, Hua and Pei, 2010b, Huang and Liu, 2009, Rintaro et al., 2002], we assume that any two disjoint subsets of Boolean variables, $X_A$ and $X_B$ of $X_E$, are conditionally independent given a subset $X_C$ ($X_A \perp X_B | X_C$), if there is a path from a vertex in $A$ to a vertex in $B$ passing through $C$. Then, the probability of a possible world graph $g'$ is given by:

$$\Pr(g \Rightarrow g') = \prod_{ne \in NS} \Pr(x_{ne}), \qquad (4.1)$$

where *NS* is all the sets of neighbor edges of *g*.

**Subgraph Isomorphism.** Given two deterministic graphs $g_1 = (V_1, E_1, \Sigma_1, L_1)$ and $g_2 = (V_2, E_2, \Sigma_2, L_2)$, we say $g_1$ is subgraph isomorphic to $g_2$ (denoted by $g_1 \subseteq_{iso} g_2$), if and only if there is an injective function $f : V_1 \rightarrow V_2$ such that:

- for any $(u, v) \in E_1$, there is an edge $(f(u), f(v)) \in E_2$;

- for any $u \in V_1$, $L_1(u) = L_2(f(u))$; and

- for any $(u, v) \in E_1$, $L_1(u, v) = L_2(f(u), f(v))$.

The subgraph $(V_3, E_3)$ of $g_2$ with $V_3 = \{f(v)|v \in V_1\}$ and $E_3 = \{(f(u), f(v))|(u, v) \in E_1\}$ is called the embedding of $g_1$ in $g_2$.

**Subgraph Isomorphism Probability.** For a deterministic graph $f$ and an uncertain graph $g$, we define their subgraph isomorphism probability (SIP) as

$$\Pr(f \subseteq_{iso} g) = \sum_{g' \in SUB(f,g)} \Pr(g \Rightarrow g'), \tag{4.2}$$

where $SUB(f, g)$ is $g$'s possible worlds that are supergraphs of $f$; that is, $SUB(f, g) = \{g' \in PWG(g)| f \subseteq_{iso} g'\}$.

**Maximum Common Subgraph (MCS).** Given two deterministic graphs $g_1$ and $g_2$, the maximum common subgraph of $g_1$ and $g_2$ is the largest subgraph of $g_2$ that is subgraph isomorphic to $g_1$, denoted by $mcs(g_1, g_2)$.

**Subgraph Distance.** Given two deterministic graphs $g_1$ and $g_2$, the subgraph distance is, $dis(g_1, g_2) = |g_1| - |mcs(g_1, g_2)|$. Here, $|g_1|$ and $|mcs(g_1, g_2)|$ denote the number of edges in $g_1$ and $mcs(g_1, g_2)$, respectively. For a distance threshold $\delta$, if $dis(g_1, g_2) \leq \delta$, we call $g_1$ is subgraph similar to $g_2$ or $g_2$ is supergraph similar to $g_1$.

Note that subgraph distance only depends on the edge set difference, which is consistent with pervious works on similarity search over deterministic graphs [He and Singh, 2006, Shang et al., 2010, Yan et al., 2005]. The operations on an edge consist of edge deletion, relabeling and insertion.

**Subgraph Similarity Probability.** For a given query graph $q$, an uncertain graph $g^2$ and a subgraph distance threshold $\delta$, we define their subgraph similarity probability as

$$\Pr(q \subseteq_{sim} g) = \sum_{g' \in SUB(q,g)} \Pr(g \Rightarrow g'), \tag{4.3}$$

where $SUB(q, g)$ is $g$'s possible world graphs and $q$ has subgraph distance to each $g' \in SUB(q, g)$ no larger than $\delta$, that is, $SUB(q, g) = \{g' \in PWG(g)| dis(q, g') \leq \delta\}$.

---

[2]Without loss of the generality, in this chapter, we assume a query graph is a connected deterministic graph, and an uncertain graph is connected.

**Probabilistic Subgraph Similarity Query**. Given a set of uncertain graphs $D = \{g_1, ..., g_n\}$, a query graph $q$, and a probability threshold $\epsilon$ ($0 < \epsilon \leq 1$), a subgraph similarity query returns a set of uncertain graphs $\{g \,|\, \Pr(q \subseteq_{sim} g) \geq \epsilon, g \in D\}$.

**Supergraph Similarity Probability**. For a given query graph $q$, an uncertain graph $g$ and a subgraph distance threshold $\delta$, we define their supergraph similarity probability as

$$\Pr(q \supseteq_{sim} g) = \sum_{g' \in SUP(q,g)} \Pr(g \Rightarrow g'), \tag{4.4}$$

where $SUP(q, g)$ is $g$'s possible world graphs that have subgraph distance to $q$ no larger than $\delta$; that is, $SUP(q, g) = \{g' \in PWG(g\,) \,|\, dis(g', q) \leq \delta\}$.

**Supergraph Similarity Probability**. Given a set of uncertain graphs $D = \{g_1, ..., g_n\}$, a query graph $q$, and a probability threshold $\epsilon$ ($0 < \epsilon \leq 1$), a supergraph similarity query returns a set of uncertain graphs $\{g \,|\, \Pr(q \supseteq_{sim} g) \geq \epsilon, g \in D\}$.

In order to answer a probabilistic subgraph or supergraph similarity query efficiently, we need to calculate the subgraph similarity probability (SUBP) or supergraph similarity probability (SUPP) efficiently. We now show the time complexities of calculating SUBP and SUPP.

**Theorem 4.1**    *It is #P-hard to calculate the subgraph similarity probability.*

**Proof Sketch.** Here we just highlight the major steps here. We consider a probabilistic graph whose edge probabilities are independent from each other. This probabilistic graph model is a special case of the probabilistic graph defined by Uncertain Graph. We prove the theorem by reducing an arbitrary instance of the #P-complete DNF counting problem [Garey and Johnson, 1979] to an instance of the problem of computing $\Pr(q \subseteq_{sim} g)$ in polynomial time. Figure 4.2 illustrates an reduction for the DNF formula $F = (y_1 \wedge y_2) \vee (y_1 \wedge y_2 \wedge y_3) \vee (y_2 \wedge y_3)$. In the figure, the graph distance between $q$ and each possible world graph $g'$ is 1 (delete vertex $w$ from $q$). Each truth assignment to the variables in $F$ corresponds to a possible world graph $g'$ derived from $g$. The probability of each truth assignment equals to the probability of $g'$ that the truth assignment corresponds to. A truth assignment satisfies $F$ if and only if $g'$, the truth assignment corresponds to, is subgraph similar to $q$ (suppose graph distance is 1). Thus, $\Pr(F)$ is equal to the probability, $\Pr(q \subseteq_{sim} g)$.

Similarly, we obtain the time complexity of calculating SUPP as follows.

**Theorem 4.2**    *It is #P-hard to calculate the supergraph similarity probability.*

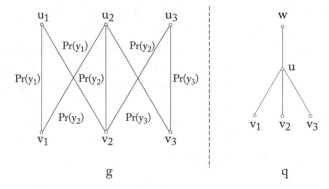

Figure 4.2: The uncertain graph $g$ and query graph $q$ constructed for $(y_1 \wedge y_2) \vee (y_1 \wedge y_2 \wedge y_3) \vee (y_2 \wedge y_3)$.

## 4.2    PROBABILISTIC SUBGRAPH SIMILARITY QUERY PROCESSING

### FRAMEWORK OF OUR APPROACH

**Structural Pruning**

The idea of structural pruning is straightforward. Formally, for $g \in D$, let $g^c$ denote the *corresponding deterministic graph* after we remove all the uncertain information from $g$. We have the following.

**Theorem 4.3**    *If $q \not\subseteq_{sim} g^c$, $\Pr(q \subseteq_{sim} g) = 0$.*

Based on this observation, given $D$ and $q$, we can prune the database $D^c = \{g_1^c, ..., g_n^c\}$ using conventional deterministic graph similar matching methods. In this chapter, we adopt the method in Yan et al. [2005] to quickly compute results. Yan et al. [2005] uses a multi-filter composition strategy to prune large number of graphs directly without performing pairwise similarity computation, which makes [Yan et al., 2005] more efficient compared to other graph similarity search algorithms [He and Singh, 2006, Zeng et al., 2009]. Assume the result is $SC_q^c = \{g^c | q \subseteq_{sim} g^c, g^c \in D^c\}$. Then, its corresponding uncertain graph set, $SC_q = \{g | g^c \in SC_q^c\}$, is the input for uncertain subgraph similarity matching in the next step.

**Probabilistic Pruning**

To further prune the results, we propose a PMI for probabilistic pruning. For a given set of uncertain graphs $D$ and its corresponding set of deterministic graphs $D^c$, we create a feature set $F$ from $D^c$, where each feature is a deterministic graph, i.e., $F \subset D^c$. In PMI, for each $g \in SC_q$, we can locate a set $D_g = \{\langle LowerB(f_j), UpperB(f_j)\rangle | f_j \subseteq_{iso} g^c, 1 \leq j \leq |F|\}$ where

*LowerB(f)* and *UpperB(f)* are the lower and upper bounds of the subgraph isomorphism probability of $f$ to $g$. If $f$ is not subgraph isomorphic to $g^c$, we have $\langle 0 \rangle$.

In the probabilistic filtering, we first determine the remaining graphs after $q$ is relaxed with $\delta$ edges, where $\delta$ is the subgraph distance threshold. Suppose the remaining graphs are $\{rq_1, ... rq_i, ... rq_a\}$. For each $rq_i$, we compute two features $f_i^1$ and $f_i^2$ in $D_g$ such that $rq_i \supseteq_{iso} f_i^1$ and $rq_i \subseteq_{iso} f_i^2$. Then, we can calculate upper and lower bounds of $\Pr(q \subseteq_{sim} g)$ based on the values of $UpperB(f_i^1)$ and $LowerB(f_i^2)$ for $1 \le i \le a$, respectively. If the upper bound of $\Pr(q \subseteq_{sim} g)$ is smaller than probability threshold $\epsilon$, $g$ is pruned. If the lower bound of $\Pr(q \subseteq_{sim} g)$ is not smaller than $\epsilon$, $g$ is in the final answers.

### Verification

In this step, we calculate $\Pr(q \subseteq_{sim} g)$ for query $q$ and candidate answer $g$, after probabilistic pruning, to make sure $g$ is really an answer, i.e., $\Pr(q \subseteq_{sim} g) \ge \epsilon$.

## PROBABILISTIC PRUNING

We first conduct structural pruning to remove uncertain graphs that do not approximately contain the query graph $q$, and then we use probabilistic pruning techniques to further filter the remaining uncertain graph set, named $SC_q$.

### Pruning Conditions

We first introduce an index structure, PMI, to facilitate probabilistic filtering. Each column of the matrix corresponds to an uncertain graph in the database $D$, and each row corresponds to an indexed feature. Each entry records $\{LowerB(f), UpperB(f)\}$, where $UpperB(f)$ and $LowerB(f)$ are the upper and lower bounds of the subgraph isomorphism probability of $f$ to $g$, respectively.

**Example 4.4**    Figure 4.3 shows the PMI of uncertain graphs in Figure 4.1. Note that the upper or lower bounds in PMI are derived from the methods proposed in Section 4.2.

Given a query $q$, an uncertain graph $g$ and subgraph distance $\delta$, we generate a graph set, $U = \{rq_1, .., rq_a\}$, by relaxing $q$ with $\delta$ edge deletions or relabelings.[3] Here, we use the solution proposed in Yan et al. [2005] to generate $\{rq_1, .., rq_a\}$. Suppose we have built the PMI. For each $g \in SC_q$, in PMI, we locate

$$D_g = \{\langle LowerB(f_j), UpperB(f_j) \rangle | f_j \subseteq_{iso} g^c, 1 \le j \le |F|\}.$$

For each $rq_i$, we find two graph features in $D_g$, $\{f_i^1, f_i^2\}$, such that $rq_i \supseteq_{iso} f_i^1$ and $rq_i \subseteq_{iso} f_i^2$, where $1 \le i \le a$. Then we have probabilistic pruning conditions as follows.

---

[3]According to the subgraph similarity search, insertion does not change the query graph.

| Feature \ Graph | 001 | 002 |
|---|---|---|
| $f_1$ | $(0.55, 0.64)$ | $(0.42, 0.5)$ |
| $f_2$ | $(0.3, 0.48)$ | $(0.26, 0.58)$ |
| $f_3$ | $0$ | $(0.08, 0.15)$ |

PMI

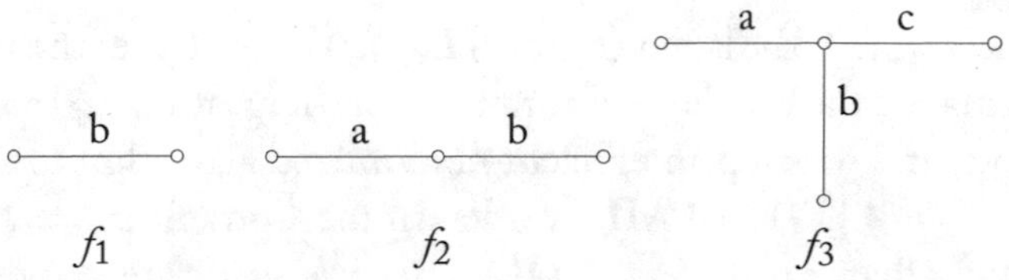

Features

Figure 4.3: Probabilistic matching tree of the graph $ug$ in Figure 4.1.

**Sub-Pruning 1.** Given a probability threshold $\epsilon$ and $D_g$, if $\sum_{i=1}^{a} UpperB(f_i^1) < \epsilon$, then $g$ can be safely pruned from $SC_q$.

**Sub-Pruning 2.** Given a probability threshold $\epsilon$ and $D_g$, if $\sum_{i=1}^{a} LowerB(f_i^2) - \sum_{1 \le i,j \le a} UpperB \ (f_i^2) Upper \ B(f_j^2) \ge \epsilon$, then $g$ is in the final answers, i.e., $g \in A_q$, where $A_q$ is the final answer set.

### Obtain Tightest Bounds of Subgraph Similarity Probability

In pruning conditions, for each $rq_i$ $(1 \le i \le a)$, we find only one pair of features $\{f_i^1, f_i^2\}$, among $|F|$ features, such that $rq_i \supseteq_{iso} f_i^1$ and $rq_i \subseteq_{iso} f_i^2$. Then we compute the upper bound, $U_{sim}(q) = \sum_{i=1}^{a} UpperB(f_i^1)$ and the lower bound $L_{sim}(q) = \sum_{i=1}^{a} LowerB(f_i^2) - \sum_{1 \le i,j \le a} UpperB(f_i^2) \ UpperB(f_j^2)$. However, there are many $f_i^1$s and $f_i^2$s satisfying conditions among $F$ features, therefore, we can compute a large number of $U_{sim}(q)$s and $L_{sim}(q)$s. For each $rq_i$, if we find $x$ features meeting the needs among $|F|$ features, we can derive $x^a$ $U_{sim}(q)$s. Let $x = 10$ and $a = 10$, then there are $10^{10}$ upper bounds. The same holds for $L_{sim}(q)$. Clearly, it is unrealistic to determine the best bounds by enumerating all the possible ones, thus, in this section, we give efficient algorithms to obtain the tightest $U_{sim}(q)$ and $L_{sim}(q)$.

### Obtain Tightest $U_{sim}(q)$

For each $f_j$ $(1 \le j \le |F|)$ in PMI, we determine a graph set, $s_j$, that is a subset of $U = \{rq_1, ..., rq_a\}$, such that $rq_i \in s_j$ s.t. $rq_i \supseteq_{iso} f_j$. We also associate $s_j$ with a weight, $UpperB(f_j)$. Then we obtain $|F|$ sets $\{s_1, .., s_{|F|}\}$ with each set having a weight $w(s_j) = UpperB(f_j)$ for

$1 \leq j \leq |F|$. With this mapping, we transform the problem of computing the tightest $U_{sim}(q)$ into a *weighted set cover* problem defined as follows.

**Tightest** $U_{sim}(q)$. Given a finite set $U = \{rq_1, ..., rq_a\}$ and a collection $S = \{s_1, .., s_j, .., s_{|F|}\}$ of subsets of $U$ with each $s_j$ attached a weight $w_{s_j}$, we compute a subset $C \subseteq S$ to minimize $\sum_{s_j \in C} w(s_j)$ s.t. $\bigcup_{s_j \in C} s_j = U$.

## Obtain Tightest $L_{sim}(q)$

For lower bound $L_{sim}(q)$, the larger (tighter) $L_{sim}(q)$ is, the better the probabilistic pruning power is. Here we formalize the problem of computing the largest $L_{sim}(q)$ as an integer quadratic programming problem, and develop an efficient randomized algorithm to solve it.

For each $f_i$ $(1 \leq i \leq |F|)$ in PMI, we determine a graph set, $s_i$, that is a subset of $U = \{rq_1, ..., rq_a\}$, such that $rq_j \in s_i$ s.t. $rq_j \subseteq_{iso} f_i$. We associate $s_i$ with a pair weight of $\{LowerB(f_i), Upper\ B(f_i)\}$. Then we obtain $|F|$ sets $\{s_1, .., s_{|F|}\}$ with each set having a pair weight $\{w_L(s_i), w_U(s_i)\}$ for $1 \leq i \leq |F|$. Thus the problem of computing tightest $L_{sim}(q)$ can be formalized as follows.

**Tightest** $L_{sim}(q)$. Given a finite set $U = \{rq_1, ..., rq_a\}$ and a collection $S = \{s_1, ..., s_{|F|}\}$ of subsets of $U$ with each $s_i$ attached a pair weight $\{w_L(s_i), w_U(s_i)\}$, we compute a subsect $C \subseteq \{s_1, ..., s_{|F|}\}$ to maximize

$$\sum_{s_i \in C} w_L(s_i) - \sum_{s_i, s_j \in C} w_U(s_i)w_U(s_j),$$

s.t. $\bigcup_{s_i \in C} s_i = U$.

Associate an indicator variable, $x_{s_i}$, with each set $s_i \in S$, which takes value 1 if set $s_i$ is selected, and 0 otherwise. Then we want to:

$$Maximize \sum_{s_i \in C} x_{s_i} w_L(s_i) - \sum_{s_i, s_j \in C} x_{s_i} x_{s_j} w_U(s_i)w_U(s_j)$$

$$s.t. \sum_{rq \in s_i} x_{s_i} \geq 1 \quad \forall rq \in U, \tag{4.5}$$

$$x_s \in \{0, 1\}.$$

## PROBABILISTIC MATRIX INDEX

In this section, we discuss how to obtain tight $\{LowerB(f), UpperB(f)\}$ and generate features used in the PMI. (PMI).

### Bounds of Subgraph Isomorphism Probability

Each entry of PMI gives $\{LowerB(f), UpperB(f)\}$ that plays an important role in probabilistic pruning, where $LowerB(f)$ and $UpperB(f)$ are lower and upper bounds of the subgraph isomorphic probability of $f$ to $g$. We will built an effective PMI by computing $\{LowerB(f), UpperB(f)\}$ efficiently and giving tightest values of $\{LowerB(f), UpperB(f)\}$.

### LowerB(f)

Let $Ef = \{f_1, .., f_{|Ef|}\}$ be the set of all embeddings[4] of feature $f$ in the deterministic graph $g^c$, $Bf_i$ be a Boolean variable for $1 \le i \le |Ef|$, which indicates whether $f_i$ exists in $g^c$ or not, and $\Pr(Bf_i)$ be the probability that the embedding $f_i$ exists in $g$.

For a given $Bf_i$, $\Pr(Bf_i|COR)$ is a constant, since the number of embeddings overlapping with $f_i$ in $g^c$ is constant. Now we obtain the lower bound of $\Pr(f \subseteq_{iso} g)$ as

$$LowerB(f) = 1 - \prod_{i=1}^{|IN|}[1 - \Pr(Bf_i|COR)], \tag{4.6}$$

which is only dependent on the selected $|IN|$ embeddings that do not have common parts with each other.

**Obtain Tightest Lower Bound.** We construct an undirected graph, $fG$, with each *node* representing an embedding $f_i$, $1 \le i \le |Ef|$, and a *link* connecting two *disjoint* embeddings (nodes). Note that, to avoid confusions, *nodes* and *links* are used for $fG$, while *vertices* and *edges* are for graphs. We also assign each node a weight, $-\ln[1 - \Pr(Bf_i|COR)]$. In $fG$, a *clique* is a set of nodes such that any two nodes of the set are adjacent. We define the weight of a clique as the sum of node weights in the clique. Clearly, given a clique in $fG$ with weight $v$, $LowerB(f)$ is $1 - e^{-v}$. Thus, the larger the weight, the tighter (larger) the lower bound. To obtain a tight lower bound, we should find a clique whose weight is largest, which is exactly the *maximum weight clique* problem. Here we use the efficient solution in Balas and Xue [1996] to solve the maximum clique problem, and the algorithm returns the larg-est weight $z$. Therefore, we use $1 - e^{-z}$ as the tightest value for $LowerB(f)$.

### UpperB(f)

First, we define *Embedding Cut*: For a feature $f$, an embedding cut is a set of edges in $g^c$ whose removal will cause the absence of all $f$'s embeddings in $g^c$. An embedding cut is minimal if no proper subset of the embedding cut is an embedding cut. In this chapter, we use minimal embedding cut.

Denote an embedding cut by $c$ and its corresponding Boolean variable (same as $Bf$) by $Bc$, where $Bc$ is true indicating that the embedding cut $c$ exists in $g^c$. It is not difficult to obtain

$$\begin{aligned}\Pr(f \subseteq_{iso} g) &= 1 - \Pr\left(Bc_1 \vee ... \vee Bc_{|Ec|}\right) \\ &= \Pr\left(\overline{Bc_1} \wedge ... \wedge \overline{Bc_{|Ec|}}\right),\end{aligned} \tag{4.7}$$

where $Ec = \{c_1, ..., c_{|Ec|}\}$ is the set of all embedding cuts of $f$ in $g^c$. Equation (4.7) shows that the subgraph isomorphism probability of $f$ to $g$ equals the probability of all $f$'s embedding cuts disappearing in $g$.

---

[4]In this chapter, we use the algorithm in Yan and Han [2003] to compute embeddings of a feature in $g^c$.

For *Lower* $B(f)$, we can rewrite Equation (4.7) as follows:

$$
\begin{aligned}
\Pr\left(f \subseteq_{iso} g\right) &= \Pr\left(\overline{Bc_1} \wedge ... \wedge \overline{Bc_{|Ec|}}\right) \\
&\leq \Pr\left(\overline{Bc_1} \wedge ... \wedge \overline{Bc_{|IN'|}} | \overline{Bc_{|IN'|+1}} \wedge ... \wedge \overline{Bc_{|Ec|}}\right) \\
&= \prod_{i=1}^{|IN'|}\left[1 - \Pr\left(Bc_i | \overline{Bc_{|IN'|+1}} \wedge ... \wedge \overline{Bc_{|Ec|}}\right)\right] \\
&= \prod_{i=1}^{|IN'|}\left[1 - \Pr\left(Bc_i | \overline{Bc_1} \wedge ... \wedge \overline{Bc_{|D|}}\right)\right] \\
&= \prod_{i=1}^{|IN'|}\left[1 - \Pr\left(Bc_i | COM\right)\right],
\end{aligned}
\tag{4.8}
$$

where $IN' = \{Bc_1, ..., Bc_{|IN'|}\}$ is a set of Boolean variables whose corresponding cuts are disjoint, $COM = \overline{Bc_1} \wedge ... \wedge \overline{Bc_{|D|}}$, and the corresponding cut of $Bc_j \in D = \{Bc_1, ..., Bc_{|D|}\}$ has common parts with the corresponding cut of $Bc_i$.

Finally, we obtain the upper bound as

$$
UpperB(f) = \prod_{i=1}^{|IN'|}\left[1 - \Pr\left(Bc_i | COM\right)\right].
\tag{4.9}
$$

The upper bound only relies on the picked embedding cut set in which any two cuts are disjoint.

*Calculation of Embedding Cuts* We build a connection between embedding cuts in $g^c$ and cuts for two vertices in a deterministic graph.

Suppose $f$ has $|Ef|$ embeddings in $g^c$, and each embedding has $k$ edges. Assign $k$ labels, $\{e_1, ..., e_k\}$, for edges of each embedding (the order is random.). We create a corresponding *line* graph for each embedding by (1) creating $k + 1$ *isolated* nodes, and (2) connecting these $k + 1$ nodes to be a line by associating $k$ edges (with corresponding labels) of the embedding. Based on these line graphs, we construct a *parallel* graph, $cG$. The node set of $cG$ consists of all nodes of the $|Ef|$ line graphs and two new nodes, $s$ and $t$. The edge set of $cG$ consists of all edges (with labels) of the $|Ef|$ line graphs. In addition, one edge (without label) is placed between an end node of each line graph and $s$. Similarly, there is an edge between $t$ and the other end node of each line graph. As a result, $|Ef|$ embeddings are transformed into a deterministic graph $cG$.

Based on this transformation, we have the following.

**Theorem 4.5** *The embedding cut set of $g^c$ is also the cut set (without edges incident to $s$ and $t$) from $s$ to $t$ in $cG$.*

In this work, we determine embedding cuts using the method in Karzanov and Timofeev [1986].

**Example 4.6**    Figure 4.4 shows the transformation for feature $f_2$ in graph 002 in Figure 4.1. In $cG$, we can find cuts $\{e_2, e_4\}$, $\{e_1, e_3, e_4\}$, and $\{e_2, e_3\}$ which are clearly the embedding cuts of $f_2$ in 002.

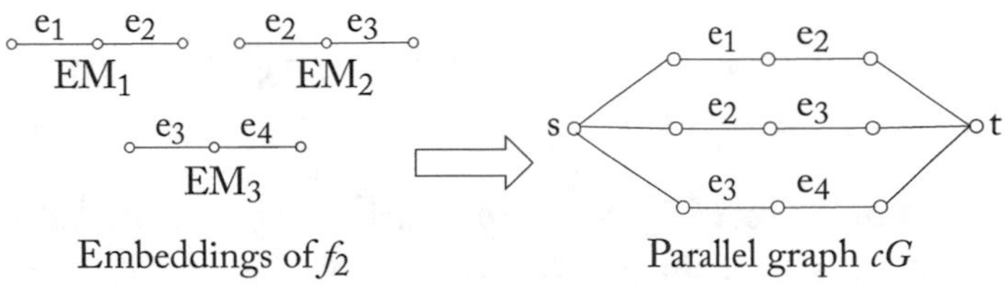

Figure 4.4: Transformation from embeddings of $f_2$ to parallel graph $cG$.

**Feature Generation**

We would like to select frequent and discriminative features to construct a PMI.

To achieve this, we consider $UpperB(f)$ given in Equation (4.9), since the upper bound plays a most important role in the pruning capability. According to Equation (4.9), to get a tight upper bound, we need a large disjoint cut set and a large $\Pr(Bc_i|COM)$. Suppose the cut set is $IN''$. Note that $|IN''| = |IN'|$, since a cut in $IN''$ has a corresponding Boolean variable $Bc_i$ in $IN'$. From the calculation of embedding cuts, it is not difficult to see that a large number of disjoint embeddings leads to a large $|IN''|$. Thus, we would like a feature that has a large number of disjoint embeddings. Since $|COM|$ is small, a small size feature results in a large $\Pr(Bc_i|COM)$. In summary, we should index a feature, which complies with following rules.

**Rule 1.** Select features that have a large number of disjoint embeddings.

**Rule 2.** Select small size features.

# 4.3    PROBABILISTIC SUPERGRAPH SIMILARITY QUERY PROCESSING

## COMPARED TO SUBGRAPH SIMILARITY SEARCH

In subgraph similarity search, we propose to effectively filter uncertain data graphs (i.e., prune false answers and validate true answers) without computing subgraph similarity probability. Specifically, we give structural and probabilistic pruning rules to filter out uncertain graphs. However, these pruning rules have no indication on $\Pr(q \supseteq_{sim} g)$.

We first examine the structural pruning rule: If $q \not\supseteq_{sim} g^c$, $\Pr(q \supseteq_{sim} g) = 0$. This rule does not work correctly for probabilistic supergraph similarity search.

## LIGHT WEIGHT FILTERING TECHNIQUES

We propose a feature-based probabilistic pruning condition that is easy to implement and can filter out false uncertain graphs quickly. Next, we give a feature generation algorithm that can pick out powerful graph features.

**Pruning Rules**

**Theorem 4.7**   *Given an uncertain graph $g$, a query $q$, and a graph feature $f$ of $g^c$, suppose that $f \not\subseteq_{sim} q$. Then, $\Pr(q \supseteq_{sim} g) \leq 1 - \Pr(f \subseteq_{sim} g)$.*

**Proof.** Let $A$ denote the set of PWGs $g'$ of $g$ such that $g' \subseteq_{sim} q$, and $B$ denote the set of PWGs $g'$ of $g$ such that $f \subseteq_{sim} g'$. Since $g' \subseteq_{sim} q$ and $f \not\subseteq_{sim} q$, $f \not\subseteq_{sim} g'$ and $A = \{g'|g' \subseteq_{sim} q, f \not\subseteq_{sim} g'\}$. Then $A \subseteq PWG(g) - B$, and we have:

$$
\begin{aligned}
\Pr(q \supseteq_{sim} g) &= \sum_{g' \in A} \Pr(g') \\
&\leq \sum_{g' \in PWG(g')} \Pr(g') - \sum_{g' \in B} \Pr(g') \qquad (4.10) \\
&= 1 - \Pr(f \subseteq_{sim} g).
\end{aligned}
$$

If we use the Inequality in (4.10) as a pruning rule, we should calculate $\Pr(q \subseteq_{sim} g)$ efficiently. However, according to Theorem 4.1, it is NP-hard to calculate $\Pr(f \subseteq_{sim} g)$. To solve the problem, we have the following probabilistic pruning rule.

**Super-Pruning 1.** Given an uncertain graph $g$, a query $q$, a threshold $\epsilon$ and a graph feature $f$ such that $f \not\subseteq_{sim} q$, if $\Pr(q \supseteq_{sim} g) \leq 1 - \Pr(f \subseteq_{sim} g) \leq 1 - \sum_{i=1}^{a} LowerB(f_i^2) + \sum_{1 \leq i,j \leq a} UpperB(f_i^2)Upper\,B(f_j^2) < \epsilon$, then $g$ can be safely pruned from the database $D$.

**Feature Generation**

The feature based index $I$ consists of frequent subgraphs $F$ from $D^c$. However, there might exist thousands or millions of features, and it would be unrealistic to index all of them. Thus, our goal is to maximize the pruning capability of $I$ with a small number of indexed features. Motivated by machine learning methods for query processing [Seshadri and Swami, 1995, Stonebraker, 1989], in this section, we employ a model, which uses a query log as the training data, to select features offline. Based on the model, we develop an optimal selection mechanism to remove useless features so that $I$ can have a great pruning capability.

Let $C_q$ be the candidate set after probabilistic pruning. The naive solution *SCAN*, to the supergraph similarity search problem examines the database $D$ sequentially and computes SUPP for each uncertain graph to decide whether its SUPP is not smaller than $\epsilon$. For a query $q$, we define the *gain*, $J$, of indexing a graph feature set $F$ as the number of SUPP computations that can be saved from *SCAN*:

$$J = |D| - |C_q|$$
$$= |\cup_{q \doteq CND} \{g|g \in D\}|, \qquad (4.11)$$

where $CND \triangleq UpperB < \epsilon$.

To obtain more effective features, we use a set of queries $\{q_1, q_2, ..., q_a\}$ instead of a single query. In this case, an optimal index should maximize the total gain

$$J_{total} = \sum_{l=1}^{a} |\cup_{q_l \doteq CND} \{g|g \in D\}|, \qquad (4.12)$$

which is the summation of the gain in Equation (4.11) over all queries.

We map the problem of maximizing Equation (4.12) to the maximum coverage as follows.

**Feature Generation.** Given a set of supergraph queries $Q = \{q_1, ..., q_a\}$ and its corresponding set of uncertain graph databases $\{D_1, ..., D_a\}$, we relate a feature $f$ in the frequent subgraph set $F_0 = \{f_1, ..., f_b\}$ to a set of uncertain graphs $G_f = \{g|f \subseteq_{iso} g, g \in D_i \, for 1 \leq i \leq a\}$, if the uncertain graph $g$ (indexed by $f$) is pruned in the probabilistic pruning (i.e., *CND*). We want to select $F \subset F_0$ such that $|\cup_{f \in F} G_f|$ is maximized.

## STRONG FILTERING TECHNIQUES

The filtering technique given in Super-Pruning 1 can remove false uncertain graphs efficiently. But we do not know how close the upper bound in Pruning 1 comes to the true value. In other words, we do not know how effective the pruning power is. Thus, in this section, we prove a formula that can calculate the true value of SUPP. Next, we give a strong pruning condition derived from the formula.

We first define *maximal common subgraph*. When two graphs have subgraphs that are isomorphic, then these subgraphs are called common subgraphs. An MCS is a common subgraph which has the maximal number of edges, in other words, if $s$ is a common subgraph of graphs $h_1$ and $h_2$, and there is no other common subgraph which has more edges than $s$, then $s$ is a maximal common subgraph of $h_1$ and $h_2$. Note that two graphs may have many MCSs. For example, Figure 4.5 shows two graphs $g$ and $q$, and Figure 4.6 gives four MCSs between $g$ and $q$.

Next, for an MCS $MG$ between $q$ and $g^c$, we define a Boolean variable $Bmg$. $Bmg$ is true if $MG$ appears in the graph $g^c$ and $Pr(Bmg)$ is the probability that $Bmg$ is true. Let $w$ be the number of all MCSs between $q$ and $g^c$. For SUPP, we have the following.

**Lemma 4.8**

$$Pr(q \supseteq_{sim} g) = Pr(Bmg_1 \vee Bmg_2 \vee ... \vee Bmg_w). \qquad (4.13)$$

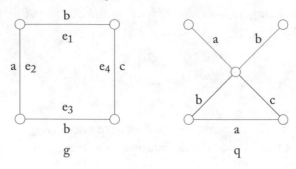

Figure 4.5: Uncertain graph and supergraph query.

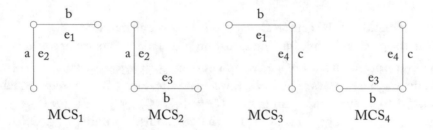

Figure 4.6: Maximal common subgraphs between $g$ and $q$ in Figure 4.5.

The PWGs of $g$ that have fewer edges may be subgraph similar to $q$, though $g^c$ is not subgraph similar to $q$. Thus, the MCS $MG_i$ may not appear in $g^c$, in other words, $Bmg_i$ may be false. Recall that $w$ is the total number of MCSs. Then we have $Bmg_0 \lor \ldots \lor Bmg_{|E(g)|} = Bmg_1 \lor \ldots \lor Bmg_{|w|}$. From the above equation, we can obtain the conclusion.

Lemma 4.8 gives a method to compute SUPP. The intuition is as follows: For the uncertain supergraph matching, each possible graph $g'$ of $g$ relaxes a distance threshold into a set of graphs $g''$, and then $g''$ subgraph matches query $q$. Note that both $g''$ and $g'$ are subgraphs of $g$. A result of $g''$ subgraph matches $q$, say $r$, is a subgraph of $q$. Thus, $r$ is a MCS of $q$ and $g'$. If all possible graphs of $g$ conduct the above process, we obtain all MCSs between $q$ and $g$. Therefore, the probability of $q$ being supergraph similar to $g$ equals the probability that at least one MCS between $q$ and $g^c$ appears in $g$. Figure 4.5 shows an uncertain graph $g$ and a query $q$. The four MCSs shown in Figure 4.6 contribute to SUPP, i.e., $\Pr(q \supseteq_{sim} g) = \Pr(MCS_1 \lor MCS_2 \lor MCS_3 \lor MCS_4)$.

Lemma 4.8 indicates a major difference between calculating SUBP and SUPP. We give an example to illustrate this. For SUBP, if $q$ is not subgraph similar to $g^c$, the value of SUBP is 0 (in this case, $q$ is not subgraph similar to any PWG of $g$). In contrast to SUPP, if $q$ is not supergraph similar to $g^c$, the value of SUPP may be larger than 0 (in this case, many PWGs of $g$ may be subgraph similar to $q$). In fact, the MCSs between $q$ and $g$ contribute to SUPP in the case of $q \not\supseteq_{sim} g^c$. The example also shows that the value of SUPP is usually large. In conclusion, MCS leads to difficulties of computing SUPP.

Based on Lemma 4.8, we obtain the following pruning rules in analogy to subgraph similarity search.

Given a query $q$, an uncertain graph $g$ and a distance threshold $\delta$, we generate the MCS set, $U = \{MG_1, .., MG_a\}$ between $q$ and $g^c$. Here, we use the solution proposed in Koch [2001] to generate $\{MG_1, .., MG_a\}$. We also use the index, PMI, for subgraph similarity search (Section 4.2). Then for each $g \in D$, in PMI, we locate $D_g = \{\langle LowerB(f_j), UpperB(f_j)\rangle \mid f_j \subseteq_{iso} g^c, 1 \le j \le |F|\}$. For each $MG_i$, we find two graph features in $D_g$, $\{f_i^1, f_i^2\}$, such that $MG_i \supseteq_{iso} f_i^1$ and $MG_i \subseteq_{iso} f_i^2$, where $1 \le i \le a$. Then we have novel pruning conditions as follows.

**Super-Pruning 2.** Given a probability threshold $\epsilon$ and $D_g$, if $\sum_{i=1}^{a} UpperB(f_i^1) < \epsilon$, then $g$ can be pruned from $D$.

**Super-Pruning 3.** Given a probability threshold $\epsilon$ and $D_g$, if $\sum_{i=1}^{a} LowerB(f_i^2) - \sum_{1 \le i,j \le a} UpperB(f_i^2)UpperB(f_j^2) \ge \epsilon$, then $g$ is in the final answers, i.e., $g \in A_q$, where $A_q$ is the final answer set.

To strengthen the two pruning rules, we use the techniques in Section 4.2 to obtain tight $UpperB(f)$ and $Lower-B(f)$.

To obtain effective features for Super-Pruning 2 and 3, we extend the feature generation algorithm for Super-Pruning 1. In Super-Pruning 1, one graph feature is used to prune an uncertain graph, but in Super-Pruning 2 and 3, a set of graph features is used to filter out an uncertain graph. Therefore, we can use a set of features instead of one feature to obtain the new feature generation algorithm.

**Sets of Features Generation.** Given a set of supergraph queries $Q = \{q_1, ..., q_a\}$ and its corresponding set of uncertain graph databases $\{D_1, ..., D_a\}$, we relate a set of features $F' = \{f_1, ..., f_a\} \subset F_0 = \{f_1, ..., f_b\}$ to a set of uncertain graphs $G_{F'}$, if the uncertain graph $g \in G'_F$ is pruned in the probabilistic pruning (i.e., Super-Pruning 2 and 3). We want to select a collection $C$ of subsets of $F_0$ such that $|\cup_{F' \in C} G_{F'}|$ is maximized.

Finally, we obtain graph features: $\bigcup_{F' \in C} F'$.


## VERIFICATION

In this section, we present the algorithms to compute $\Pr(q \supseteq_{sim} g)$ for each $g \in C_q$. Then we can obtain the query answers, i.e., $A_q = \{g \mid \Pr(q \supseteq_{sim} g) \ge \epsilon\}$. As shown in Theorem 4.2, calculating SUPP is a #P-hard problem, so we use sampling methods to get an approximate result.

**Basic Sampling**

In this subsection, we give a basic sampling algorithm based on Monte Carlo theory.

During the sampling process, we sample $N$ *possible world graphs*, $g_1, g_2, \ldots, g_N$, according to $\Pr(x_{ne})$ of each neighbor edge set. Then, on each sampled possible world graph $g_i$, we check whether $q$ is supergraph similar to $g_i$. We set a flag $y_i$ for each $g_i$, so that

$$y_i = \begin{cases} 1 & \text{if } q \text{ is supergraph similar to } g_i \\ 0 & \text{otherwise} \end{cases}.$$

Thus, the estimator $\widehat{\theta}$ equals to

$$\widehat{\theta} = \widehat{\Pr(q \supseteq_{sim} g)} = \frac{\sum_{i=1}^{N} y_i}{N}. \tag{4.14}$$

For any sampling method, the MSE incorporates both bias and precision of an estimator $\widehat{\theta}$ into a measure of overall accuracy. It is calculated as

$$MSE(\widehat{\theta}) = E[(\widehat{\theta} - \theta)^2] = Var(\widehat{\theta}) + Bias(\widehat{\theta}, \theta).$$

The bias of an estimator is given by

$$Bias(\widehat{\theta}) = E(\widehat{\theta}) - \theta.$$

An estimator of $\theta$ is unbiased if its bias is 0 for all values of $\theta$, that is, $E(\widehat{\theta}) = \theta$. As the estimator of Monte Carlo method is unbiased Fishman [1991], thus,

$$MSE(\widehat{\theta}) = Var(\widehat{\theta}) = \frac{1}{N}\theta(1 - \theta) \approx \frac{1}{N}\widehat{\theta}(1 - \widehat{\theta}), \tag{4.15}$$

where $\theta = \Pr(q \supseteq_{sim} g)$.

**Advanced Sampling**

In the basic sampling, we should increase the value of $N$ if we want to guarantee an accurate answer. But as a consequence, the calculation will take a long time. To solve the problem, in this subsection, we propose an advanced sampling algorithm that can obtain an accurate answer efficiently.

The main idea of the advanced sampling is to sample a lot of possible world graphs together in one sampling. Thus, we can reduce $N$ compared with the basic sampling. Below, we use an example to show the idea.

**Example 4.9**    Figure 4.5 shows an uncertain graph $g$ and a query $q$ with distance threshold $\delta = 1$. Figure 4.7 shows five possible world graphs (PWG) that are subgraph similar to $q$. These PWGs contain the graph $e_1 e_2$ or its subgraphs $e_1$ and $e_2$. The graph $e_1 e_2$ is a MCS between $q$ and

$g^c$. According to Lemma 4.8, the MCS $e_1 e_2$ contributes to the SUPP of $q$ to $g$. In the advanced sampling, we apply the MCS detection algorithm to sample edges $e_1 e_2$, and the five PWGs are totally the PWGs that contain $e_1 e_2$ or its subgraphs $e_1$ and $e_2$. Thus, our advanced sampling algorithm only needs one sampling process that samples all these five PWGs together. But in the basic sampling algorithm, it takes five times to sample them. In other words, sampling once in the advanced algorithm has the same effect with sampling five times in the basic algorithm. Thus, by together sampling the PWGs containing the same MCS, the advanced sampling algorithm can effectively reduce the sample size $N$.

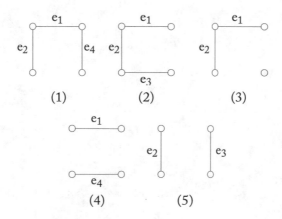

Figure 4.7: Advantage of advanced sampling method.

# SUMMARY

In this chapter, we study the problem of similarity graph containment queries (subgraph and supergraph similarity queries) on large uncertain graphs with correlation on edge probability distributions. Although it is an NP-hard problem to answer the subgraph or supergraph similarity query, we employ a filter-and-verify methodology to answer the two queries efficiently. During the filtering phase, for the subgraph similarity query, we first propose a PMI with tight upper and lower bounds of subgraph isomorphism probability. Then based on PMI, we derive upper and lower bounds of the subgraph similarity probability, while for supergraph similarity query, we compute effective bounds of supergraph similarity probability based on maximal common subgraphs of query and uncertain graph. Therefore, we are able to filter out a large number of uncertain graphs without calculating the subgraph and supergraph similarity probabilities. During verification to fast validate final answers, we use the Inclusion-Exclusion principle to develop sampling algorithms for the subgraph similarity query, while we develop sampling algorithms based on the Horvitz-Thompson estimator for supergraph queries.

CHAPTER 5

# Influence Maximization

In recent years, social networks have found increasing popularity because of their ability to connect geographically disparate groups of individuals. Much of its benefit is embedded in the information flows in social networks. These information flows arise as a result of the communication between different entities in the network. Social networks, in fact, have advantages as a medium for fast, widespread information cascade as in the case of the announcement of death of Michael Jackson [DeBolt, 2009]. They can serve as a medium to collectively achieve a social goal. For example, with the use of groups and event pages in Facebook and Twitter, events such as "Day of Action" quickly reached to the thousands of protestors [Garrison and Knoll, 2008]. The information flow is also impacted by the network topology and the intensity of information flow interactions between different nodes. Since information flows play such a key role in the popularity of social networks, significant research has been performed in recent years to characterize important properties of such flows. Indeed, it has been verified by user study and market research [Bond et al., 2012, Iyengar et al., 2011] that campaigners should identify influential users based on their centrality in the social network. We first discuss various information diffusion models, and then introduce the problem of identifying the most influential users considering several factors.

## 5.1 INFORMATION DIFFUSION MODELS

We describe two widely used information diffusion models from the literature, namely the independent cascade (IC) and the linear threshold (LT) models [Kempe et al., 2003]. In both of them, a social network $\mathcal{G}$ is modeled as a triple $(V, E, p)$, where $V$ is a set of $n$ nodes, $E \subseteq V \times V$ is a set of $m$ directed edges, and $p : E \to (0, 1)$ is a probability function that assigns a probability to each edge in $E$. The probability $p_{uv}$ on a directed edge $(u, v) \in E$ represents the probability that node $v$ adopts a product due to the influence of node $u$, because $u$ adopted that product before. When $v$ adopts that product, it automatically becomes eligible to influence its neighbors who has not adopted that product already.

**IC Model.** In the IC model, the campaign starts with an initially active (i.e., adopted her product) set of seed nodes, and then unfolds in discrete steps. When some node $u$ first becomes active at step $t$, it gets a single chance to activate each of its currently inactive out-neighbors $v$; it succeeds with probability $p_{u,v}$. If $u$ succeeds, then $v$ will become active at step $t + 1$. Whether or not $u$ succeeds at step $t$, it cannot make any further attempts in the subsequent rounds. If a node $v$ has incoming edges from multiple newly activated nodes, their attempts are sequenced in an arbitrary order. Also, each node can be activated only once and it stays active until the end. The campaigning process runs until no more activations are possible.

**LT Model.** In the LT model, each node $v$ has an activation threshold $\theta_v \leq 1$. In addition, there is a constraint that the sum of the probabilities of all incoming edges for every node must be at most 1. The campaign starts with an initially active set of seed nodes, and then unfolds in discrete steps. If the sum of the probabilities of the incoming edges from all active nodes is greater than or equal to the activation threshold of an inactive node, then the node gets activated in the next round. Each node can only be activated once and stays active until the end.

In addition to IC and LT models, various other information diffusion models were proposed in the literature, e.g., game theoretic models [Dubey et al., 2006], Markov Random Field models [Domingos and Richardson, 2001], viral propagation models [Gallos et al., 2010], and continuous-time diffusion models [G.-Rodriguez et al., 2011]. The information cascading process is also known as the word-of-mouth recommendation, and it has a great potentiality in viral marketing as discussed below.

## 5.2   THE INFLUENCE MAXIMIZATION PROBLEM

In viral marketing, whenever a social network user buys a product, she is viewed as being influenced or activated. The classical viral marketing problem identifies the top-$k$ seed users in a social network such that the expected number of influenced users in the network, starting from those seed users and following some influence cascading model, is maximized. The budget $k$ on the seed-set size usually depends on the campaigner. In other words, it depends on how many initial users the campaigner can directly influence to buy her product by advertisements, giving free samples and discounted prices.

Domingos and Richardson [2001] formulate influence maximization as an optimization problem, while Kempe et al. [2003] proposes the IC and the LT models, as well as designs approximation algorithms with provable performance guarantees. Since then, several heuristics have been proposed to improve the efficiency of that method [Chen et al., 2010, Goyal et al., 2011a,b, Kim et al., 2013, Leskovec et al., 2007]. Very recently, Borgs et al. [2014] and Tang et al. [2014] developed almost linear-time influence maximization algorithms, while ensuring the same approximation guarantee as Kempe et al. [2003]'s original method. Below we provide a summary of the pioneering work by Kempe et al. [2003].

The problem of identifying the top-$k$ seed nodes $S$ that maximize the expected spread $\sigma(S)$ in the network, by following IC or LT model, is NP-hard [Kempe et al., 2003]. However, it was shown in the paper that the objective function $\sigma(S)$ is non-negative, monotonic, and submodular with respect to inclusion of seed nodes. Therefore, an iterative hill-climbing algorithm that greedily selects the seed node at every iteration which brings the maximum marginal gain to the expected spread can produce a solution with performance guarantee $(1 - \frac{1}{e}) \approx 0.63$, where $e$ is the base of the natural logarithm [Nemhauser et al., 1978]. More precisely, assuming that a set $S$ of seed users has been already computed, at next iteration the algorithm selects a seed user

$v^*$ such that:

$$v^* = \underset{v \in V \setminus S}{argmax} \left[ \sigma \left( S \cup \{c\} \right) - \sigma \left( S \right) \right]. \tag{5.1}$$

Given a seed set $S$, unfortunately there is no efficient way to compute the expected spread $\sigma(S)$. Kempe et al. claimed that finding an efficient algorithm for computing $\sigma(S)$ is open. Instead of an exact algorithm, they employed MC sampling to estimate the expected spread. Therefore, in essence, their algorithm produces a solution within $(1 - \frac{1}{e} - \epsilon)$ of the optimal influence spread, where $\epsilon$ depends on the accuracy of the MC estimate of influence spread given a seed set. Later, it has been proved that the problem of computing the expected spread, by following IC model, is indeed #**P**-hard [Chen et al., 2010].

**Reverse Sketching.** Reverse sketching-based influence maximization algorithms, first proposed in Borgs et al. [2014] and later improved in Tang et al. [2014, 2015], have become the state-of-the-art methods with both good scalability and an $(1 - 1/e - \epsilon)$ approximation guarantee. Let $G$ denote a (deterministic) sub-graph of the input uncertain graph $\mathcal{G}$, generated by removing each edge $e \in E$ with probability $1 - p(e)$ independently. The *Reverse Reachable (RR) Set* for a random node $v$ consists of all nodes that can reach $v$ in $G$.

The workflow of the reverse sketching is as follows.

1. Generate $\theta$ random RR-sets from $\mathcal{G}$ .

2. Next, a greedy algorithm repeatedly identifies the node presenting in the majority of RR-sets, adds it to the seed set, and the RR-sets containing it are removed. This process continues until $k$ seed nodes are identified.

In Tang et al. [2014], it was proved that when $\theta$ is sufficiently large, reverse sketching returns near-optimal results with high probability.

**Varieties of Influence Maximization Problem.** Several varieties of the influence maximization problem has been considered, e.g., Lappas et al. [2010], introduces the concept of *target marketing* and $k$-effectors—by identifying $k$ seed nodes such that a given activation pattern can be established. The notion of target marketing is also considered in Li et al. [2011] that maximizes influence over a region of the network. Viral marketing in the presence of a *negative campaign* is investigated in Bharathi et al. [2007] and Carnes et al. [2007]. These works assume that the later campaign has prior knowledge of rival side's initial seed nodes. Borodin et al. [2010] analyzes the similar problem under the LT model while Chen et al. [2011] and Budak et al. [2011] attempt at preventing the spread of an existing negative campaign in the network. Recently, Tzoumas et al. [2012] studies the viral marketing problem between *non-cooperative* campaigns who select seeds alternatively. However, *competitive* new products from rival companies are often launched around the same time. Thus, Li et al. [2015a], Goyal and Kearns [2012], and Lu et al. [2013] consider viral marketing in the presence of multiple competing campaigners, who promote their products in a social network around the same time. Lu et al. [2015] studies *co-operative* influence maximization in the presence of multiple complementary products. *Influence maximization as a service*, provided by the social network host is discussed in Lu et al.

[2013] and Khan et al. [2016]. *Topic-aware* influence maximization is introduced in Chen et al. [2015], Barbieri et al. [2012], and Aslay et al. [2014]. Maximization of *product adoption* is studied in Bhagat et al. [2012] and Li et al. [2015b]. Influence maximization in dynamic graphs is investigated in Ohsaka et al. [2016] and Song et al. [2017]. There are also works on learning the influence network and cascades, e.g., Cheng et al. [2014], Feng et al. [2018], Goyal et al. [2010], Kutzkov et al. [2013], and Goyal et al. [2011a]. In addition to viral marketing, recently influence maximization has been employed in community search [Mehmood et al., 2016] and in finding influential nodes for integration in brain networks [Ferraro et al., 2018]. For a detailed survey on influence maximization, the readers may look at Agrawal et al. [2011a], Aslay et al. [2018], Chen et al. [2013], and Agrawal et al. [2011b].

Next, we shall briefly introduce three variants of the classical influence maximization problems—(a) information diffusion in the presence of a competing/ negative cascade, (b) influence maximization as a service provided by the social network host, and (c) the topic-aware influence maximization problem.

## 5.3    COMPETITIVE INFLUENCE MAXIMIZATION

As stated earlier, several variants of competitive influence maximization were considered in the past. We shall highlight two of them. Chen et al. [2011] studies when adoption of a product creates both positive and negative influence among users; and therefore, both these types of influence propagate in the network. Budak et al. [2011], on the other hand, designs algorithms to prevent the spread of an existing negative campaign by introducing a competing positive campaign.

Chen et al. [2011] introduces a variation of the IC model, called the IC-N model. Each node can be in one of the three states—neutral, positive, or negative. Discrete time steps are used to model dynamic changes in the network. We say that a node $v$ is activated at time $t$ if it is positive or negative at time $t$, and was neutral at time $(t - 1)$. The model has a parameter $q$ called the *quality factor*, which indicates the probability that a node stays positive after it is activated by a positive in-neighbor. Initially at time $t = 0$, all nodes in a pre-determined seed set $S \subset V$ are activated, and for each node $v \in S$, with probability $q$, $v$ becomes positive and with probability $(1 - q)$, it becomes negative. At a time $t > 0$, for any neutral node $v$, let $A_t(v) \subseteq N^{in}(v)$ be the set of in-neighbors of $v$ that were activated at time $(t - 1)$. Every node $u \in A_t(v)$ tries to activate $v$ with an independent probability of $p_{u,v}$. If one of them is successful, $v$ is activated at step $t$. Moreover, if $v$ is activated by a negative node $u$, then $v$ becomes negative; if $v$ is activated by a positive node $u$, then with probability $q$, $v$ becomes positive, while with probability $(1 - q)$, it becomes negative. To determine which node activates $v$, we randomly permute all nodes in $A_t(v)$, and let each node in $A_t(v)$ try to activate $v$ following the permutation order until we find the first node $u$ that successfully activates $v$. Once $v$ is activated and fixed its state (either positive or negative), it does not change its state any more. The activation process stops when there is no new activated node in a time step. Clearly, if $q = 1$, nodes can only be positively activated, and IC-N is reduced to the original IC model. The influence maximization problem in this setting, is to find a seed set of size $k$ such that the expected positive influence spread in the network is maximized. Chen et al. [2011] showed that the objective function is non-negative, monotonic, and sub-modular with respect to the seed set. Therefore, an iterative hill climbing method as earlier will produce an approximate solution with performance guarantee $(1 - \frac{1}{e} - \epsilon)$ of the optimal positive influence spread.

Budak et al. [2011] proposes the multi-campaigner IC (MCIC) model, which follows the same process as IC, except two major differences. First, if some node $u$ is activated with campaign of $C_i$, it attempts to activate its out-neighbors $v$ with the campaign of $C_i$. Second, an activated node $v$ adopts one campaign uniformly at random from all its in-neighbors which were successfully activated in the last round. Each node can be activated only once and by only one of the campaigns; also the node stays activated with that campaign until the end. Therefore, the MCIC model assumes the following influence cascading scenario: people adopt a product when they come in direct contact with their friends who very recently adopted that product. Given an existing negative campaign, the objective is to select $k$ seed nodes for the positive campaign such that we can prevent maximum number of users from adopting the ongoing negative campaign. The authors have demonstrated sub-modularity of the objective function in the presence of *high effectiveness* property of the positive campaign, that is, the edge probabilities for the positive information diffusion is always 1. In such a scenario, an iterative hill climbing method will produce an approximate solution with performance guarantee $(1 - \frac{1}{e} - \epsilon)$.

## 5.4   INFLUENCE MAXIMIZATION AS A SERVICE

The bulk of the research in the domain of viral marketing assumes that the social network structure is available to the campaigners. However, in real-world scenarios, the social network platforms are owned by third-party hosts [Lu et al., 2013], such as Facebook, Twitter, and LinkedIn; and the hosts keep their social graphs secret for their own benefits and for privacy reasons. Therefore, marketing companies themselves are not able to select their best seed sets due to lack of access to the social network graph.

Therefore, Lu et al. [2013] assumes that the seed set selections are done by the social network host on behalf of her clients, who are the marketing campaigners. In real-world, multiple companies compete and they launch comparable products around the same time (e.g., Nintendo's Wii vs. Sony's Playstation vs. Microsoft's X-Box; Microsoft's Surface vs. Apple's iPad vs. Samsung Note 3). Thus, the host often needs to run multiple competing viral marketing campaigns together over the network. However, due to various product-adoption costs, it is very unlikely that an average user will purchase more than one of the competing products. Since most of the users adopt only one of the competing products, it implies that the seed sets of the competing campaigners require to be mutually non-overlapping. Lu et al. [2013] studies the problem of selecting seed nodes for each campaigner such that the expected spread of each campaign over the network is balanced in a fair manner.

Khan et al. [2016], on the other hand, introduces the problem of maximizing the revenue of the social network host by selling multiple viral marketing campaigns to its campaigners. In particular, the authors assume that the campaigners would be willing to spend their overall budget for viral marketing into two parts. Each campaigner informs the host about: (a) her budget on the seed-set size (i.e., the number of seed users, $k$), and also (b) how much money she is willing to pay to the host for each of her target users if that user adopts her product. While the campaigner might not know the exact social network structure, it is usually easier for her to define her target users, either explicitly, or via some constraints, e.g., people in the age group 20–30, all banking professionals, etc. The campaigner allocates a small $k$ as the number of her seed nodes to whom she is willing to provide free samples, discounted price, etc. She uses rest of her budget to pay the social network host according to the agreement, which can be a small amount of money for each of her target users who adopts her product. In this setting, a natural incentive for the social network host will be how to select the seeds for her client campaigners such that her overall expected revenue considering all clients is maximized. It has been shown in the paper that the objective function is NP-hard, and neither monotonic, nor sub-modular with respect to seed sets. However, the authors developed various approximate algorithms with theoretical performance guarantees under certain additional constraints.

## 5.5   TOPIC-AWARE INFLUENCE MAXIMIZATION

Many problem variants of influence maximization have been considered in the literature, majority of them assuming that the influence cascade probabilities between two users are fixed and without taking into consideration the actual information being cascaded. Users generally apply tags to characterize their contents in an online social network, e.g., hashtags in *Twitter* and *Instagram*. Moreover, one can identify representative keywords (e.g., the most frequent ones after removing stop words) from the contents, and use them as tags. The probability that a tweet originated by a user $u$ will be re-tweeted by her follower $v$ clearly depends on the hashtags and other keywords in that tweet (Figure 5.1 [Li et al., 2008]). Following an empirical study by Barbieri and Bonchi over the real-world *Last.FM* social network [Barbieri and Bonchi, 2014], a new song due to collaboration between *Lana del Rey* and *Katy Perry* would reach to more people (by means of information diffusion), than some other song that combines *Metal* and *Electronic* bands. In the context of 2016 U.S. Presidential election, Hillary Clinton's campaign promises were infrastructure rebuild, free trade, open borders, unlimited immigration, equal pay, increasing minimum wage, etc. To get more votes, Hillary's publicity manager could have prioritized the most influential among all these standpoints in speeches, while also planning how to influence more voters from the "blue wall" states (Michigan, Pennsylvania, and Wisconsin) [Sieff, 2016]. As speeches should be kept limited due to time constraints and risk of becoming ineffective because of information overload, it is desirable to find a limited set of standpoints that maximize the influence from a set of early adopters (e.g., popular people who are close to Hillary Clinton) to a set of target voters (e.g., citizens of the "blue wall" states) [Li et al., 2017].

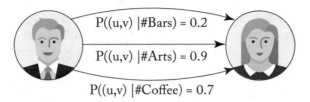

Figure 5.1: Edge influence probabilities based on information topics.

The classic influence maximization problem has been recently considered in a topic-aware fashion [Aslay et al., 2014, Barbieri et al., 2012, Chen et al., 2015]. Both Aslay et al. [2014] and Chen et al. [2015] aim at finding a set of seed nodes that maximize the spread of information for a *given* topic set. In Barbieri and Bonchi [2014], introduce the problem of identifying the top-$k$ seed nodes, together with finding the optimal topic distribution. Very recently, Li et al. [2017] explores a user's most influential topic set in a social network. Ke et al. [2018] and Khan et al. [2018] investigate the problem of jointly finding the top-$k$ seed users and top-$r$ relevant tags for targeted influence maximization in a social network. They designed an iterative, heuristic algorithm that alternatively optimizes the top-$k$ seeds and the top-$r$ tags, until it converges to a local optimum.

## SUMMARY

In this chapter we introduce various information diffusion models over social networks, the classical influence maximization problem and its variants, as well as a brief overview of the competitive influence maximization problem, influence maximization as a service, and the topic-aware influence maximization problem.

# CHAPTER 6

# Major Open Problems

With the availability of uncertain networks and their applications in real world, the last ten years has seen an unprecedented interest and research in designing algorithms for querying and mining of uncertain graphs. There are yet many questions that need to be investigated. We conclude this book by highlighting some future research directions.

**Finding One Good Possible World.** Majority of the work on uncertain graphs resorts to sampling a sufficient number of independent possible worlds for estimating the probability that a certain property holds, e.g., graph similarity. While there are many algorithmic advances [Zhu et al., 2015] on efficient sampling (e.g., off-line sampling) as well as more effective post-processing (e.g., BFS sharing), one still requires in the order of thousands of independent samples in order to achieve a reasonable accuracy [Jin et al., 2011b, Khan et al., 2014]. In a recent work by Parchas et al. [2014], the authors studied the problem of finding only one "good" possible world so that one can still preserve the underlying graph properties as much as possible. In particular, the paper analyzed the problem of preserving the degree distribution of the uncertain graph by generating just one good possible world. This introduces a new direction to deal with uncertain graphs: *Is it possible to pre-compute one good possible world for various kinds of uncertain graph queries?* More work [Song et al., 2016] is necessary to define good possible worlds and identify them; and this could be an interesting framework to speed up uncertain graphs processing.

**Trade-off between Accuracy vs. Efficiency.** Since an exact computation is often infeasible over large-scale uncertain graphs, there is a trade-off between scalability and efficiency vs. accuracy in uncertain graphs processing [Fu et al., 2017]. Hence, it is important to identify the application areas and their specific requirements, e.g., efficiency vs. effectiveness, false positive vs. false negative rates, cost of probing uncertain edges, etc., and the algorithm-specific parameters to tune these results. As an example, if some application requires finding the reliable set with a higher precision, one can use the reliable path-based approach instead of more expensive sampling techniques [Khan et al., 2014].

**Advanced Graph Queries and Analytics.** With the emergence of large-scale uncertain graph applications, it is also important to re-define the semantics and algorithms for many classical graph operations, e.g., graph partitioning and summarization [Hassanlou et al., 2013], centrality [III and Neville, 2011], sparsification [Parchas et al., 2018], and graph visualization [Vehlow et al., 2013]. Unfortunately, there is not much work on such advanced queries and analytics over uncertain graphs. It is also important to consider uncertain graph problems, e.g., information diffusion in the context of more complex network structure, such as higher-order networks [Benson et al., 2016] and multi-layer graphs [Kivela et al., 2014].

**Systems for Uncertain Graphs.** Many big-graph startups came out in the past few years, such as Gephi, FlockDB, GraphBuilder, HypergraphDB, AllegroGraph, Gremlin, and Neo4J. They usually provide their own open-source tools, APIs, and graph databases. However, these big-graph startups hardly support any uncertainty features. On the other hand, various uncertain database prototypes exist, mainly in the context of relational data, e.g., DeepDive [Shin et al., 2015], BayesStore [Wang et al., 2008], and PrDB [Sen et al., 2009]. It would be interesting to look at system specific challenges of uncertain graphs processing, and whether the aforementioned uncertain databases are good fits for dealing with uncertain graphs. It would also be interesting to analyze whether it is more beneficial to incorporate uncertainty features on the native graph databases provided by today's big-graph startups. Another interesting direction could be to look at distributed graph processing paradigms [Cheng et al., 2015, Zou et al., 2017], e.g., PREGEL [Malewicz et al., 2010], GraphLab [Low et al., 2012], GraphX [Gonzalez et al., 2014], and Arabesque [Teixeira et al., 2015], as well as modern hardware including FPGA and GPU to accelerate uncertain graphs querying.

**Ground-Truths and Open-Source Softwares.** It is important to identify standard datasets, ground-truths, and benchmarks for uncertain graph queries and systems. As an example, while tremendous algorithmic advances have been made in the area of influence maximization in social networks with viral marketing as its main application, to date the research has seen a modest penetration in industry-strength viral marketing case studies [Castillo et al., 2012]. The primary reason could be lack of ground-truths on how information cascade occurs over social networks. In addition, lack of standard datasets, open-source softwares, and benchmarks is often a challenging problem in terms of comparing with previous works.

# Bibliography

E. Adar and C. Re. Managing uncertainty in social networks. *IEEE Data Engineering Bulletin*, 30(2):15–22, 2007. 1, 3

C. C. Aggarwal. *Managing and Mining Uncertain Data*. Springer, 2009. DOI: 10.1007/978-0-387-09690-2 1

C. C. Aggarwal and P. S. Yu. A Survey of uncertain data algorithms and applications. *IEEE Transactions on Knowledge and Data Engineering*, 21(5):609–623, 2009. DOI: 10.1109/tkde.2008.190 10

K. K. Aggarwal, K. B. Misra, and J. S. Gupta. Reliability evaluation: A comparative study of different techniques. *Microelectronics Reliability* 14(1):49–56, 1975. DOI: 10.1016/0026-2714(75)90461-8 10, 11

D. Agrawal, C. Budak, and A. E. Abbadi. Information diffusion in social networks: Observing and affecting what society cares about. In *CIKM*, 2011a. DOI: 10.1145/2063576.2064036 58

D. Agrawal, C. Budak, and A. E. Abbadi. Information diffusion in social networks: Observing and influencing societal interests. *PVLDB*, 4(12):1512–1513, 2011b. DOI: 10.1145/2063576.2064036 58

A. Arora, S. Galhotra, and S. Ranu. Debunking the myths of influence maximization: An in-depth benchmarking study. In *SIGMOD*, 2017. DOI: 10.1145/3035918.3035924 10

Ç. Aslay, N. Barbieri, F. Bonchi, and R. A. B.-Yates. Online topic-aware influence maximization queries. In *EDBT*, 2014. DOI: 10.14778/2735703.2735706 10, 58, 61

Ç. Aslay, L. V. S. Lakshmanan, W. Lu, and X. Xiao. Influence maximization in online social networks. In *WSDM*, 2018. DOI: 10.1145/3159652.3162007 58

S. Asthana, O. King, F. Gibbons, and F. Roth. Predicting protein complex membership using probabilistic network reliability. *Genome Research*, 14:1170–1175, 2004. DOI: 10.1101/gr.2203804 1

S. Auer, C. Bizer, G. Kobilarov, J. Lehmann, R. Cyganiak, and Z. Ives. DBpedia: A nucleus for a Web of open data. In *ISWC*, 2007. DOI: 10.1007/978-3-540-76298-0_52 3

E. Balas and J. Xue. Weighted and unweighted maximum clique algorithms with upper bounds from fractional coloring. *Algorithmica*, 15:397–412, 1996. DOI: 10.1007/s004539900022 31, 45

M. O. Ball. Computational complexity of network reliability analysis: An overview. *IEEE Transactions on Reliability*, 35(3):230–239, 1986. DOI: 10.1109/tr.1986.4335422 12, 13

N. Barbieri and F. Bonchi. Influence maximization with viral product design. In *SDM*, 2014. DOI: 10.1137/1.9781611973440.7 60, 61

N. Barbieri, F. Bonchi, and G. Manco. Topic-aware social influence propagation models. In *ICDM*, 2012. DOI: 10.1109/icdm.2012.122 5, 58, 61

A. R. Benson, D. F. Gleich, and J. Leskovec. Higher-order organization of complex networks. *Science*, 353(6295):163–166, 2016. DOI: 10.1126/science.aad9029 64

S. Bhagat, A. Goyal, and L. V. S. Lakshmanan. Maximizing product adoption in social networks. In *WSDM*, 2012. DOI: 10.1145/2124295.2124368 58

S. Bharathi, D. Kempe, and M. Salek. Competitive influence maximization in social networks. In *WINE*, 2007. DOI: 10.1007/978-3-540-77105-0_31 57

C. Bishop. *Pattern Recognition and Machine Learning*. Springer, 2006. 7

G. O. Blog. Introducing the Knowledge Graph: Thing, not Strings. http://googleblog.blogspot.com/2012/05/introducing-knowledge-graph-things-not.html, 2012. 3

P. Boldi, F. Bonchi, A. Gionis, and T. Tassa. Injecting uncertainty in graphs for identity obfuscation. *PVLDB*, 5(11):1376–1387, 2012. DOI: 10.14778/2350229.2350254 1

K. Bollacker, C. Evans, P. Paritosh, T. Sturge, and J. Taylor. Freebase: A collaboratively created graph database for structuring human knowledge. In *SIGMOD*, 2008. DOI: 10.1145/1376616.1376746 1, 3

F. Bonchi, F. Gullo, A. Kaltenbrunner, and Y. Volkovich. Core decomposition of uncertain graphs. In *KDD*, 2014. DOI: 10.1145/2623330.2623655 3, 10

R. M. Bond, C. J. Fariss, J. J. Jones, A. D. I. Kramer, C. Marlow, J. E. Settle, and J. H. Fowler. A 61-million-person experiment in social influence and political mobilization. *Nature*, 489 (7415):295–298, 2012. DOI: 10.1038/nature11421 55

C. Borgs, M. Brautbar, J. T. Chayes, and B. Lucier. Maximizing social influence in nearly optimal time. In *SODA*, 2014. DOI: 10.1137/1.9781611973402.70 56, 57

A. Borodin, Y. Filmus, and J. Oren. Threshold models for competitive influence in social networks. In *WINE*, 2010. DOI: 10.1007/978-3-642-17572-5_48 57

T. B. Brecht and C. J. Colbourn. Lower bounds on two-terminal network reliability. *Discrete Applied Mathematics*, 21(3):185–198, 1988. DOI: 10.1016/0166-218x(88)90065-0 14

C. Budak, D. Agrawal, and A. E. Abbadi. Limiting the spread of misinformation in social networks. In *WWW*, 2011. DOI: 10.1145/1963405.1963499 57, 58, 59

D. Bulka and J. B. Dugan. Network s-t reliability bounds using a 2-dimensional reliability polynomial. *IEEE Transactions on Reliability*, 43(1):39–45, 1994. DOI: 10.1109/24.285106 14

T. Carnes, C. Nagarajan, S. M. Wild, and A. v. Zuylen. Maximizing influence in a competitive social network: A follower's perspective. In *ICEC*, 2007. DOI: 10.1145/1282100.1282167 57

C. Castillo, W. Chen, and L. V. S. Lakshmanan. Information and influence spread in social networks. In *KDD*, 2012. DOI: 10.2200/s00527ed1v01y201308dtm037 64

L. Chen and C. Wang. Continuous subgraph pattern search over certain and uncertain graph streams. *IEEE Transactions on Knowlsdge and Data Engineering*, 22(8):1093–1109, 2010. DOI: 10.1109/tkde.2010.67 3

S. Chen, J. Fan, G. Li, J. Feng, K. l. Tan, and J. Tang. Online topic-aware influence maximization. *PVLDB*, 8(6):666–677, 2015. DOI: 10.14778/2735703.2735706 10, 58, 61

W. Chen, C. Wang, and Y. Wang. Scalable influence maximization for prevalent viral marketing in large-scale social networks. In *KDD*, 2010. DOI: 10.1145/1835804.1835934 56, 57

W. Chen, A. Colin, R. Cumming, T. Ke, Z. Liu, D. Rincon, X. Sun, Y. Wang, W. Wei, and Y. Yuan. Influence maximization in social networks when negative opinions may emerge and propagate. In *SDM*, 2011. DOI: 10.1137/1.9781611972818.33 57, 58, 59

W. Chen, L. V. S. Lakshmanan, and C. Castillo. *Information and Influence Propagation in Social Networks*. Synthesis Lectures on Data Management. Morgan & Claypool Publishers, 2013. DOI: 10.2200/s00527ed1v01y201308dtm037 58

Y. Chen and D. Z. Wang. Knowledge expansion over probabilistic knowledge bases. In *SIGMOD*, 2014. DOI: 10.1145/2588555.2610516 1, 3

J. Cheng, L. A. Adamic, P. A. Dow, J. M. Kleinberg, and J. Leskovec. Can cascades be predicted? In *WWW*, 2014. DOI: 10.1145/2566486.2567997 58

Y. Cheng, Y. Yuan, L. Chen, and G. Wang. The reachability query over distributed uncertain graphs. In *ICDCS*, 2015. DOI: 10.1109/icdcs.2015.109 64

H. N. Chui, W.-K. Sung, and L. Wong. Exploiting indirect neighbors and topological weight to predict protein function from protein-protein interactions. *Bioinformatics*, 22(13):47–58, 2007. DOI: 10.1093/bioinformatics/btl145 38

J. B. Collins and S. T. Smith. Network discovery for uncertain graphs. In *Fusion*, 2014. 6

T. H. Cormen, C. Stein, R. L. Rivest, and C. E. Leiserson. *Introduction to Algorithms*, 2nd ed. McGraw-Hill Higher Education, 2001. DOI: 10.2307/2583667 21

CPR, EMBL, SIB, KU, TUD, and UZH. STRING. http://string-db.org/ 1, 2

M. Dallachiesa, C. C. Aggarwal, and T. Palpanas. Node classification in uncertain graphs. In *SSDBM*, 2014. DOI: 10.1145/2618243.2618277 3, 10

V. DeBolt. Michael Jackson on TMZ, Iran on Twitter. http://www.blogher.com/spreading-news, 2009. 55

A. Deshpande, L. Getoor, and P. Sen. Graphical models for uncertain data. In Springer, Ed., *Managing and Mining Uncertain Data*, 2009. DOI: 10.1007/978-0-387-09690-2_4 10

P. Domingos and M. Richardson. Mining the network value customers. In *KDD*, 2001. DOI: 10.1145/502512.502525 3, 10, 56

P. Dubey, R. Garg, and B. D. Meyer. Competing for customers in a social network: The quasi-linear case. In *WINE*, 2006. DOI: 10.1007/11944874_16 56

D. Hochbaum, Ed. *Approximation Algorithms for NP-Hard Problems*. PWS, 1997. DOI: 10.4171/owr/2004/28 32

W. Fan, J. Li, S. Ma, N. Tang, and Y. Wu. Adding regular expressions to graph reachability and pattern queries. In *ICDE*, 2011. DOI: 10.1109/icde.2011.5767858 26, 28

S. Feng, G. Cong, A. Khan, X. Li, Y. Liu, and Y. M. Chee. Inf2vec: Latent representation model for social influence embedding. In *ICDE*, 2018. 58

G. D. Ferraro, A. Moreno, B. Min, F. Morone, U. P.-Ramirez, L. P.-Cervera, L. C. Parra, A. Holodny, S. Canals, and H. A. Makse. Finding influential nodes for integration in brain networks using optimal percolation theory. *Nature Communications*, 9(2274), 2018. DOI: 10.1038/s41467-018-04718-3 58

G. S. Fishman. A comparison of four Monte Carlo methods for estimating the probability of s-t connectedness. *IEEE Transactions on Reliability*, 35(2):145–155, 1986. DOI: 10.1109/tr.1986.4335388 14, 17

G. S. Fishman. A Monte Carlo sampling plan based on product form estimation. In *Proc. of the 23rd Conference on Winter Simulation*, pages 1012–1017, IEEE Computer Society, 1991. DOI: 10.1109/wsc.1991.185717 32, 52

National Center for Biotechnology Information. NCBI. http://www.ncbi.nlm.nih.gov/ 1

L. Foschini, J. Hershberger, and S. Suri. On the complexity of time-dependent shortest paths. In *SODA*, 2011. DOI: 10.1007/s00453-012-9714-7 3

H. Frank. Shortest paths in probabilistic graphs. *Operational Research*, 17:583–599, 1969. DOI: 10.1287/opre.17.4.583 2

X. Fu, Z. Xu, Q. Peng, L. Fu, and X. Wang. Complexity vs. optimality: Unraveling source-destination connection in uncertain graphs. In *INFOCOM*, 2017. DOI: 10.1109/infocom.2017.8057094 63

M. G.-Rodriguez, D. Balduzzi, and B. Schölkopf. Uncovering the temporal dynamics of diffusion networks. In *ICML*, 2011. 56

L. Gallos, S. Havlin, M. Kitsak, F. Liljeros, H. Makse, L. Muchnik, and H. Stanley. Identification of influential spreaders in complex networks. *Nature Physics*, 6(11):888–893, 2010. DOI: 10.1038/nphys1746 56

J. Galtier, A. Laugier, and P. Pons. Algorithms to evaluate the reliability of a network. In *DRCN*, 2005. DOI: 10.1109/drcn.2005.1563849 14

M. R. Garey and D. S. Johnson. *Computers and Intractability: A Guide to the Theory of NP-Completeness*. W. H. Freeman, 1979. DOI: 10.1137/1024022 26, 31, 40

J. Garrison and C. Knoll. Prop. 8 Opponents Rally across California to Protest Gay-Marriage Ban. *Los Angeles Times*, 2008. 55

J. Ghosh, H. Q. Ngo, S. Yoon, and C. Qiao. On a routing problem within probabilistic graphs and its application to intermittently connected networks. In *INFOCOM*, 2007. DOI: 10.1109/infcom.2007.201 5

J. Gonzalez, R. Xin, A. Dave, D. Crankshaw, M. J. Franklin, and I. Stoica. GraphX: Graph processing in a distributed dataflow framework. In *OSDI*, 2014. 64

A. Goyal, F. Bonchi, and L. V. S. Lakshmanan. Learning influence probabilities in social networks. In *WSDM*, 2010. DOI: 10.1145/1718487.1718518 58

A. Goyal, F. Bonchi, and L. V. S. Lakshmanan. A data-based approach to social influence maximization. *PVLDB*, 5(1):73–84, 2011a. DOI: 10.14778/2047485.2047492 56, 58

A. Goyal, W. Lu, and L. V. S. Lakshmanan.    CELF++: Optimizing the greedy algorithm for influence maximization in social networks.    In *WWW*, 2011b. DOI: 10.1145/1963192.1963217 56

S. Goyal and M. Kearns.    Competitive contagion in networks.    In *STOC*, 2012. DOI: 10.1145/2213977.2214046 57

G. Hardy, C. Lucet, and N. Limnios.    K-terminal network reliability measures with binary decision diagrams.    *IEEE Transactions on Reliability*, 56(3):506–515, 2007. DOI: 10.1109/tr.2007.898572 11

N. Hassanlou, M. Shoaran, and A. Thomo. Probabilistic Graph Summarization, *WAIM*. 2013. 63

H. He and A. K. Singh.  Closure-tree: An index structure for graph queries. In *ICDE*, 2006. DOI: 10.1109/icde.2006.37 39, 41

J. Hu, B. Yang, C. Guo, and C. S. Jensen.  Risk-aware path selection with time-varying, uncertain travel costs: A time series approach.  *VLDB Journal*, 27(2):179–200, 2018. DOI: 10.1007/s00778-018-0494-9 3

M. Hua and J. Pei.  Probabilistic path queries in road networks: Traffic uncertainty aware path selection. In *EDBT*, 2010a. DOI: 10.1145/1739041.1739084 1, 3

M. Hua and J. Pei.  Probabilistic path queries in road networks: Traffic uncertainty aware path selection. In *EDBT*, 2010b. DOI: 10.1145/1739041.1739084 38

H. Huang and C. Liu. Query evaluation on probabilistic RDF databases. In *WISE*, 2009. DOI: 10.1007/978-3-642-04409-0_32 3, 38

Joseph J. Pfeiffer III and Jennifer Neville. Methods to determine node centrality and clustering in graphs with uncertain structure. In *ICWSM*, 2011. 63

R. Iyengar, C. Van den Bulte, and T. W. Valente. Opinion leadership and social contagion in new product diffusion. *Marketing Science*, 30(2):195–212, 2011. DOI: 10.1287/mksc.1100.0566 55

R. Jin, L. Liu, and C. C. Aggarwal. Discovering highly reliable subgraphs in uncertain graphs. In *KDD*, 2011a. DOI: 10.1145/2020408.2020569 3, 15

R. Jin, L. Liu, B. Ding, and H. Wang. Distance-constraint reachability computation in uncertain graphs. *PVLDB*, 4(9):551–562, 2011b. DOI: 10.14778/2002938.2002941 2, 5, 11, 14, 15, 16, 17, 25, 33, 63

R. M. Karp and M. G. Luby. A new Monte-Carlo method for estimating the failure probability of an n-component system. *Technical Report UCB/CSD-83-117*, EECS Department,
University of California, Berkeley, 1983. 17, 20

A. V. Karzanov and E. A. Timofeev. Efficient algorithm for finding all minimal edge
cuts of a nonoriented graph. *Cybernetics and Systems Analysis*, 22(2):156–162, 1986. DOI:
10.1007/bf01074775 47

V. Kassiano, A. Gounaris, A. N. Papadopoulos, and K. Tsichlas. Mining uncertain graphs: An
overview. In *Algorithmic Aspects of Cloud Computing*, 2017. DOI: 10.1007/978-3-319-57045-
7_6 10

X. Ke, A. Khan, , and G. Cong. Finding seeds and relevant tags jointly: For targeted influence
maximization in social networks. In *SIGMOD*, 2018. DOI: 10.1145/3183713.3199670 10,
61

D. Kempe, J. M. Kleinberg, and E. Tardos. Maximizing the spread of influence through a social
network. In *KDD*, 2003. DOI: 10.1145/956755.956769 1, 3, 10, 15, 55, 56

A. Khan, F. Bonchi, A. Gionis, and F. Gullo. Fast reliability search in uncertain graphs. In
*EDBT*, 2014. 2, 14, 15, 18, 63

A. Khan, B. Zehnder, and D. Kossmann. Revenue maximization by viral marketing: A social
network host's perspective. In *ICDE*, 2016. DOI: 10.1109/icde.2016.7498227 57, 60

A. Khan, F. Bonchi, F. Gullo, and A. Nufer. Conditional reliability in uncertain graphs. *IEEE
Transactions on Knowledge and Data Engineering*, 2018. DOI: 10.1109/tkde.2018.2816653 61

J. Kim, S.-K. Kim, and H. Yu. Scalable and parallelizable processing of influence maximization
for large-scale social networks? In *ICDE*, 2013. DOI: 10.1109/icde.2013.6544831 56

M. Kivela, A. Arenas, M. Barthelemy, J. P. Gleeson, Y. Moreno, and M. A. Porter. Multilayer
networks. *Journal of Complex Networks*, 2(3):203–271, 2014. DOI: 10.1093/comnet/cnu016
64

I. Koch. Enumerating all connected maximal common subgraphs in two graphs. *Theoretical
Computer Science*, 250(1):1–30, 2001. DOI: 10.1016/s0304-3975(00)00286-3 51

X. Kong, A. B. Ragin, X. Wang, and P. S. Yu. Discriminative feature selection for uncertain
graph classification. In *SDM*, 2013. DOI: 10.1137/1.9781611972832.10 3

N. J. Krogan, G. Cagney, H. Yu, G. Zhong, and X. Guo. Global landscape of protein com-
plexes in the yeast saccharomyces cerevisiae. *Nature*, 440:637–643, 2006. DOI: 10.1038/na-
ture04670 1

S. K. Thompson. *Sampling*, 3rd ed. Wiley Series in Probability and Statistics, Wiley, 2012. DOI: 10.1002/9781118162934 34

K. Kutzkov, A. Bifet, F. Bonchi, and A. Gionis. STRIP: Stream learning of influence probabilities. In *KDD*, 2013. DOI: 10.1145/2487575.2487657 58

D. L.-Nowell and J. Kleinberg. The link prediction problem for social networks. In *CIKM*, 2003. DOI: 10.1145/956958.956972 1

T. Lappas, E. Terzi, D. Gunopulos, and H. Mannila. Finding effectors in social networks. In *KDD*, 2010. DOI: 10.1145/1835804.1835937 57

J. Leskovec, J. Kleinberg, and C. Faloutsos. Graphs over time: Densification laws, shrinking diameters and possible explanations. In *KDD*, 2005. DOI: 10.1145/1081870.1081893 10

J. Leskovec, A. Krause, C. Guestrin, C. Faloutsos, J. VanBriesen, and N. Glance. Cost-effective outbreak detection in networks. In *KDD*, 2007. DOI: 10.1145/1281192.1281239 56

F.-H. Li, C.-T. Li, and M.-K. Shan. Labeled influence maximization in social networks for target marketing. In *SocialCom/PASSAT*, 2011. DOI: 10.1109/passat/socialcom.2011.152 57

H. Li, S. S. Bhowmick, J. Cui, Y. Gao, and J. Ma. GETREAL: Towards realistic selection of influence maximization strategies in competitive networks. In *SIGMOD*, 2015a. DOI: 10.1145/2723372.2723710 57

H. Li, S. S. Bhowmick, A. Sun, and J. Cui. Conformity-aware influence maximization in online social networks. *VLDB Journal*, 24(1):117–141, 2015b. DOI: 10.1007/s00778-014-0366-x 10, 58

R.-H. Li, J. X. Yu, R. Mao, and T. Jin. Efficient and accurate query evaluation on uncertain graphs via recursive stratified sampling. In *ICDE*, 2014. DOI: 10.1109/icde.2014.6816709 3, 17

X. Li, L. Guo, and Y. E. Zhao. Tag-based social interest discovery. In *WWW*, 2008. DOI: 10.1145/1367497.1367589 60

Y. Li, J. Fan, D. Zhang, and K.-L. Tan. Discovering your selling points: Personalized social influential tags exploration. In *SIGMOD*, 2017. DOI: 10.1145/3035918.3035952 17, 61

X. Lian and L. Chen. Efficient query answering in probabilistic RDF graphs. In *SIGMOD*, 2011. DOI: 10.1145/1989323.1989341 3

J. C. Liu, X. Q. Shang, Y. Meng, and M. Wang. Mining maximal dense subgraphs in uncertain PPI network. *Applied Mechanics and Materials*, 135:609–615, 2011. DOI: 10.4028/www.scientific.net/amm.135-136.609 2

L. Liu, R. Jin, C. C. Aggarwal, and Y. Shen. Reliable clustering on uncertain graphs. In *ICDM*, 2012. DOI: 10.1109/icdm.2012.11 2, 10

Y. Low, D. Bickson, J. Gonzalez, C. Guestrin, A. Kyrola, and J. M. Hellerstein. Distributed GraphLab: A framework for machine learning and data mining in the cloud. *PVLDB*, 5(8): 716–727, 2012. DOI: 10.14778/2212351.2212354 64

W. Lu, F. Bonchi, A. Goyal, and L. V. S. Lakshmanan. The bang for the buck: Fair competitive viral marketing from the host perspective. In *KDD*, 2013. DOI: 10.1145/2487575.2487649 57, 59

W. Lu, W. Chen, and L. V. S. Lakshmanan. From competition to complementarity: Comparative influence diffusion and maximization. *PVLDB*, 9(2):60–71, 2015. DOI: 10.14778/2850578.2850581 57

G. Malewicz, M. H. Austern, A. J. C. Bik, J. C. Dehnert, I. Horn, N. Leiser, and G. Czajkowski. Pregel: A system for large-scale graph processing. In *SIGMOD*, 2010. DOI: 10.1145/1807167.1807184 64

S. Maniu, R. Cheng, and P. Senellart. An indexing framework for queries on probabilistic graphs. *ACM Transactions on Database Systems*, 42(2):13:1–13:34, 2017. DOI: 10.1145/3044713 17

Y. Mehmood, F. Bonchi, and D. García-Soriano. Spheres of influence for more effective viral marketing. In *SIGMOD*, 2016. DOI: 10.1145/2882903.2915250 58

M. Mitzenmacher and E. Upfal. *Probability and Computing: Randomized Algorithms and Probabilistic Analysis*. Cambridge University Press, 2005. DOI: 10.1017/cbo9780511813603 33

W. E. Moustafa, A. Kimmig, A. Deshpande, and L. Getoor. Subgraph pattern matching over uncertain graphs with identity linkage uncertainty. In *ICDE*, 2014. DOI: 10.1109/icde.2014.6816710 5, 6

G. L. Nemhauser, L. A. Wolsey, and M. L. Fisher. An analysis of approximations for maximizing submodular set functions - I. *Mathematical Programming* 14(1):265–294, 1978. DOI: 10.1007/bf01588971 56

University of Helsinki. Biomine. `https://www.cs.helsinki.fi/group/biomine/` 1

N. Ohsaka, T. Akiba, Y. Yoshida, and K.-I. Kawarabayashi. Dynamic influence analysis in evolving networks. *PVLDB*, 9(12):1077–1088, 2016. DOI: 10.14778/2994509.2994525 10, 58

O. Papapetrou, E. Ioannou, and D. Skoutas. Efficient discovery of frequent subgraph patterns in uncertain graph databases. In *EDBT*, 2011. DOI: 10.1145/1951365.1951408 3

P. Parchas, F. Gullo, D. Papadias, and F. Bonchi.   The pursuit of a good possible world: Extracting representative instances of uncertain graphs.  In *SIGMOD*, 2014. DOI: 10.1145/2588555.2593668 15, 63

P. Parchas, N. Papailiou, D. Papadias, and F. Bonchi.  Uncertain graph sparsification. *IEEE Transactions on Knowledge and Data Engineering*, 2018. DOI: 10.1109/tkde.2018.2819651 63

J. Pearl.  Reverend Bayes on inference engines: A distributed hierarchical approach.  In *AAAI*, 1982. 10

M. Potamias, F. Bonchi, A. Gionis, and G. Kollios.  k-nearest neighbors in uncertain graphs.  In *VLDB*, 2010. DOI: 10.14778/1920841.1920967 1, 2, 5, 6, 7, 8, 11, 14, 15, 21, 22, 23, 25

J. S. Provan and M. O. Ball. The complexity of counting cuts and computing the probability that a graph is connected. *SIAM Journal of Computing*, 12:777–788, 1983. DOI: 10.1137/0212053 12

J. S. Provan and M. O. Ball.  Computing network reliability in time polynomial in the number of cuts. *Operations Research*, 32:516–526, 1984. DOI: 10.1287/opre.32.3.516 14

M. Renz, T. Bernecker, F. Verhein, A. Zuefle, and H.-P. Kriegel. Probabilistic frequent itemset mining in uncertain databases. In *KDD*, 2009. DOI: 10.1145/1557019.1557039 9

S. Rintaro, S. Harukazu, and H. Yoshihide.  Interaction generality: A measurement to assess the reliability of a protein-protein interaction. *Nucleic Acids Research*, 30(5):1163–1168, 2002. DOI: 10.1093/nar/30.5.1163 38

P. Sen, A. Deshpande, and L. Getoor.  PrDB: Managing and exploiting rich correlations in probabilistic databases. *The VLDB Journal*, 18(5):1065–1090, 2009. DOI: 10.1007/s00778-009-0153-2 64

P. Seshadri and A. N. Swami.   Generalized partial indexes.   In *ICDE*, 1995. DOI: 10.1109/icde.1995.380355 48

P. Sevon, L. Eronen, P. Hintsanen, K. Kulovesi, and H. Toivonen.  Link discovery in graphs derived from biological databases. In *DILS*, 2006. DOI: 10.1007/11799511_5 1

H. Shang, K. Zhu, X. Lin, Y. Zhang, and R. Ichise.  Similarity search on supergraph containment. In *ICDE*, 2010. DOI: 10.1109/icde.2010.5447846 39

A. Sharafat and O. Ma'rouzi.   All-terminal network reliability using recursive truncation algorithm.   *IEEE Transactions on Reliability*, 58(2):338–347, 2009. DOI: 10.1109/tr.2009.2020120 11

J. Shin, S. Wu, F. Wang, C. D. Sa, C. Zhang, and C. Ré. Incremental knowledge base construction using deepDive. *PVLDB*, 8(11):1310–1321, 2015. DOI: 10.14778/2809974.2809991 3, 64

M. Sieff. Why Hillary Clinton Lost Her Blue Wall. http://www.martinsieff.com/cycles-of-change/hillary-clinton-lost-blue-wall/, 2016. 60

G. Song, Y. Li, X. Chen, X. He, and J. Tang. Influential node tracking on dynamic social network: An interchange greedy approach. *IEEE Transactions on Knowledge and Data Engineering*, 29(2):359–372, 2017. DOI: 10.1109/tkde.2016.2620141 58

S. Song, Z. Zou, and K. Liu. Triangle-based representative possible worlds of uncertain graphs. In *DASFAA*, 2016. DOI: 10.1007/978-3-319-32049-6_18 63

M. Stonebraker. The case for partial indexes. *SIGMOD Record*, 18(4), 1989. DOI: 10.1145/74120.74121 48

F. M. Suchanek, G. Kasneci, and G. Weikum. Yago: A core of semantic knowledge. In *WWW*, 2007. DOI: 10.1145/1242572.1242667 3

D. Suciu, D. Olteanu, C. Ré, and C. Koch. *Probabilistic Databases*. Synthesis Lectures on Data Management. Morgan & Claypool Publishers, 2011. DOI: 10.2200/s00362ed1v01y201105dtm016 10

Y. Tang, X. Xiao, and Y. Shi. Influence maximization: Near-optimal time complexity meets practical efficiency. In *SIGMOD*, 2014. DOI: 10.1145/2588555.2593670 56, 57

Y. Tang, Y. Shi, and X. Xiao. Influence maximization in near-linear time: A martingale approach. In *SIGMOD*, 2015. DOI: 10.1145/2723372.2723734 10, 57

C. Taranto, N. D. Mauro, and F. Esposito. Uncertain graphs meet collaborative filtering. In *IIR*, 2012. 3

C. H. C. Teixeira, A. J. Fonseca, M. Serafini, G. Siganos, M. J. Zaki, and A. Aboulnaga. Arabesque: A system for distributed graph mining. In *SOSP*, 2015. DOI: 10.1145/2815400.2815410 64

V. Tzoumas, C. Amanatidis, and E. Markakis. A game-theoretic analysis of a competitive diffusion process over social networks. In *WINE*, 2012. DOI: 10.1007/978-3-642-35311-6_1 57

L. G. Valiant. The complexity of enumeration and reliability problems. *SIAM Journal of Computation*, 8:410–421, 1979. DOI: 10.1137/0208032 12

C. Vehlow, J. Hasenauer, A. Kramer, A. Raue, S. Hug, J. Timmer, N. Radde, F. J Theis, and D. Weiskopf. iVUN: Interactive visualization of uncertain biochemical reaction networks. *BMC Bioinformatics*, 14, 2013. DOI: 10.1186/1471-2105-14-s19-s2 63

D. Z. Wang, E. Michelakis, M. Garofalakis, and J. M. Hellerstein. BayesStore: Managing large, uncertain data repositories with probabilistic graphical models. *PVLDB*, 1(1):340–351, 2008. DOI: 10.14778/1453856.1453896 64

J. Wang, T. Kraska, M. J. Franklin, and J. Feng. CrowdER: Crowdsourcing entity resolution. In *VLDB*, 2012. DOI: 10.14778/2350229.2350263 1

W. Wu, H. Li, H. Wang, and K. Q. Zhu. Probase: A probabilistic taxonomy for text understanding. In *SIGMOD*, 2012. DOI: 10.1145/2213836.2213891 3

X. Yan and J. Han. Closegraph: Mining closed frequent graph patterns. In *KDD*, 2003. DOI: 10.1145/956755.956784 45

X. Yan, P. S. Yu, and J. Han. Substructure similarity search in graph databases. In *SIGMOD*, 2005. DOI: 10.1145/1066157.1066244 39, 41, 42

J. Y. Yen. Finding the K shortest loopless paths in a network. *Management Science*, 17(11): 712–716, 1971. DOI: 10.1287/mnsc.17.11.712 20

Y. Yuan, L. Chen, and G. Wang. Efficiently answering probability threshold-based shortest path queries over uncertain graphs. In *DASFAA*, 2010. DOI: 10.1007/978-3-642-12026-8_14 2, 8, 19

Y. Yuan, G. Wang, H. Wang, and L. Chen. Efficient subgraph search over large uncertain graphs. *PVLDB*, 4(11):876–886, 2011. 3, 5

Y. Yuan, G. Wang, L. Chen, and H. Wang. Efficient subgraph similarity search on large probabilistic graph databases. In *VLDB*, 2012. DOI: 10.14778/2311906.2311908 3, 25

Y. Yuan, G. Wang, L. Chen, and H. Wang. Graph similarity search on large uncertain graph databases. *The VLDB Journal*, 24(2):271–296, 2015. DOI: 10.1007/s00778-014-0373-y 25

Z. Zeng, A. K. H. Tung, J. Wang, L. Zhou, and J. Feng. Comparing stars: On approximating graph edit distance. *PVLDB*, 2(1):25–36, 2009. DOI: 10.14778/1687627.1687631 41

W. Zhang, X. Lin, J. Pei, and Y. Zhang. Managing uncertain data: Probabilistic approaches. In *WAIM*, 2008. DOI: 10.1109/waim.2008.42 10

H. Zhou, A. A. Shaverdian, H. V. Jagadish, and G. Michailidis. Querying graphs with uncertain predicates. In *MLG*, 2010. DOI: 10.1145/1830252.1830273 1, 3

K. Zhu, W. Zhang, G. Zhu, Y. Zhang, and X. Lin. BMC: An efficient method to evaluate probabilistic reachability queries. In *DASFAA*, 2011. DOI: 10.1007/978-3-642-20149-3_32 2, 5, 11, 14, 15, 17

R. Zhu, Z. Zou, and J. Li. Top-k reliability search on uncertain graphs. In *ICDM*, 2015. DOI: 10.1109/icdm.2015.64 14, 15, 63

L. Zou, L. Chen, and M. T. Ozsu. Distance-join: Pattern match query in a large graph database. *PVLDB*, 2(1):886–897, 2009a. DOI: 10.14778/1687627.1687727 26, 28

L. Zou, P. Peng, and D. Zhao. Top-k possible shortest path query over a large uncertain graph. In *WISE*, 2011. DOI: 10.1007/978-3-642-24434-6_6 2, 7, 8, 19, 20, 21

Z. Zou, J. Li, H. Gao, and S. Zhang. Frequent subgraph pattern mining on uncertain graph data. In *CIKM*, 2009b. DOI: 10.1145/1645953.1646028 10

Z. Zou, J. Li, H. Gao, and S. Zhang. Frequent subgraph pattern mining on uncertain graph data. In *CIKM*, 2009c. DOI: 10.1145/1645953.1646028 3, 8

Z. Zou, H. Gao, and J. Li. Discovering frequent subgraphs over uncertain graph databases under probabilistic semantics. In *KDD*, 2010a. DOI: 10.1145/1835804.1835885 1, 3, 25

Z. Zou, J. Li, H. Gao, and S. Zhang. Finding top-k maximal cliques in an uncertain graph. In *ICDE*, 2010b. DOI: 10.1109/icde.2010.5447891 2

Z. Zou, J. Li, H. Gao, and S. Zhang. Mining frequent subgraph patterns from uncertain graph data. *IEEE Transactions on Knowledge and Data Engineering*, 22(9):1203–1218, 2010c. DOI: 10.1109/tkde.2010.80 3, 25

Z. Zou, F. Li, J. Li, and Y. Li. Scalable processing of massive uncertain graph data: A simultaneous processing approach. In *ICDE*, 2017. DOI: 10.1109/icde.2017.70 64

# Authors' Biographies

## ARIJIT KHAN

**Arijit Khan** is an assistant professor in the School of Computer Engineering at Nanyang Technological University, Singapore. His research interests span in the area of big-data, big-graphs, and graph systems. He received his Ph.D. from the Department of Computer Science, University of California, Santa Barbara, and did a post-doc in the Systems group at ETH Zurich. Arijit was the recipient of the prestigious IBM Ph.D. Fellowship in 2012-13. He published several papers in premier database and data-mining conferences and journals including *SIGMOD, VLDB, TKDE, ICDE, SDM, EDBT,* and *CIKM.* Arijit co-presented tutorials on emerging graph queries, big-graph systems, summarization, and uncertain graphs at ICDE 2012, VLDB 2014, VLDB 2015, and VLDB 2017, and served in the program committee of KDD, SIGMOD, VLDB, ICDM, EDBT, WWW, and CIKM. Arijit served as the co-chair of Big-O(Q) workshop co-located with VLDB 2015.

## YUAN YE

**Yuan Ye** is now a professor in the Department of Computer Science, Northeastern University, China. His research interests are graph databases, probabilistic databases, social network analysis and big-data computing systems. Yuan Ye received the B.S., M.S., and Ph.D. degrees in Computer Science from Northeastern University in 2004, 2007, and 2011, respectively. He was a visiting scholar of the Hong Kong University of Science and Technology, the Chinese University of Hong Kong, and the University of Edinburgh. Yuan Ye published several papers in premier database conferences and journals including *SIGMOD, VLDB, ICDE, CIKM, VLDB Journal, TKDE,* and *TPDS.* He served in the program committee of *SIGMOD, VLDB, ICDE, EDBT,* and *CIKM.* Yuan Ye received the award of the CCF excellent doctoral dissertation in 2012 and the excellent youth scholar of NSFC in 2016.

## LEI CHEN

**Lei Chen** received a B.S. in Computer Science and Engineering from Tianjin University, China in 1994, an M.A. from Asian Institute of Technology, Thailand, in 1997, and a Ph.D. in Computer Science from University of Waterloo, Canada in 2005. He is now an associate professor in the Department of Computer Science and Engineering at Hong Kong University of Science and Technology. His research interests include uncertain databases, graph databases, multimedia, and time series databases, and sensor and peer-to-peer databases. He is editor-in-chief of the *VLDB Journal* and serving as an associate editor for *IEEE Transactions on Knowledge and Data Engineering* and *Distributed and Parallel Databases*. He is the PC Co-chair of the 45th International Conference on Very Large Databases (VLDB), 2019, and has served as PC Co-chair, PC Track Chair, and PC member for many conferences. He was awarded the SIGMOD Test of Time Award in 2015. He is a member of the IEEE and ACM.

Printed in the United States
by Baker & Taylor Publisher Services